My Best Poetry Unit
And Other Ideas for Teaching Poetry (Years 7-12)

Edited Ken Wats

With contributions from
Glenys Acland
Philip Allingham
Roslyn Arnold
Joe Belanger
Michael Benton
Peter Benton
Matthew Brown
John Douglas
Trevor Gambell
Jean Hayhoe
Tim Hopkins
Mark Howie
Wendy Jonas
Richard Knott
Carl Leggo
Tim Lester
Rachel Mapes
Sam Robinson
Gordon Shrubb
Ernie Tucker

PHOTOCOPIABLE

ISBN 1 876757 08 6

St Clair Press

My Best Poetry Unit And Other Ideas for Teaching Poetry (Years 7-12) is published by St Clair Press
an imprint of PHOENIX EDUCATION PTY LTD

Sydney:
PO Box 3141, Putney 2112
Tel: (02) 9809 3579 Fax: (02) 9808 1430

Melbourne:
PO Box 197, Albert Park 3206
Tel: (03) 9699 8377 Fax: (03) 9699 9242

Email: service@phoenixeduc.com
Website: www.phoenixeduc.com

Copyright © 2001 St Clair Press

Photocopying

The material in this book is copyright. The purchasing educational institution and its staff, and the individual teacher purchaser, are permitted to make copies of the pages of this book beyond their rights under the Australian Copyright Act 1968, provided that:

1. The number of copies does not exceed the number reasonably required by the educational institution to satisfy its teaching purposes;
2. Copies are made only by reprographic means (photocopying), not by electronic/digital means, and are not stored or transmitted;
3. Copies are not sold or lent.

Printing:

Printed in Australia by Five Senses Education, Seven Hills

CONTENTS

Words – Catherine Fisher   1

Part 1: My Best Poetry Unit

Performance Poetry in the Junior & Middle Secondary Years –
Jean Hayhoe, Rachel Mapes, Ken Watson   4
    The History of the Flood – John Heath-Stubbs
    The Apeman – Adrian Mitchell
    The Daniel Jazz – Vachel Lindsay
    The Young Jackaroo – Ethel Anderson
    Didjeridoo – F T Macartney
    The Song of the Whale – Kit Wright
    Junior Coaching – William Scammell
    The Mobile Rag – John Mole
    The Unquiet Grave – Anon
    Bargain Basement – F T Macartney
From Poem to Picture Book (Years 9-11) – John Douglas   17
    The Trap – Jon Stallworthy
The Editorial Committee (Years 8-11) – Ken Watson   19
    The Golden Vanity
    The Twa Corbies
    Two Ravens
    The Three Ravens
The Worst Poem in the Universe (Year 9-12) – Gordon Shrubb   26
The Poetry Detective: The Chest (Years 10-12) – Matthew Brown   28
    The Romantic Poets
Sequencing Activity (Year 9-12) – Richard Knott   34
    Green Beret – Ho Thien
Two Translations of a Chinese Poem (Years 7-10) – Glenys Acland   37
Gallery Walk (Year 9-12) – Philip Allingham   40
    Black Hull – Harry Thurston
Extended Metaphors (Year 9-10) – Wendy Jonas   43
    Portraits – Colin Thiele
    All the World's a Stage – William Shakespeare
Comparing Two Versions (Years 10-12) – Matthew Brown   47
    La Belle Dame Sans Merci – John Keats
Mapping Responses to a Poem (Years 9-12) – Michael & Peter Benton   51
    Cock-Crow – Edward Thomas
Teaching *Kubla Khan* (Years 10-12) – Ernie Tucker   53
The Pictorial Essay (Years 9-11) – Trevor Gambell & Sam Robinson   57
    White Dresses – Rhona McAdam
    At the Wedding – Andrew Wreggitt
Teaching Post-Colonial Poems (Years 9-11) – Philip Allingham   61
    History Lesson – Jeannette Armstrong
    Columbus – Robert Hull
An Introduction to Literary Theory (Years 10-12) – Mark Howie   64
    Late Fragment – Raymond Carver
    Crossing the Bar – Alfred, Lord Tennyson
    To His Coy Mistress – Andrew Marvell
    I Can't Feel the Sunshine – Lesbia Harford
Sylvia Plath: A Discussion (Years 11-12) – Tim Lester   78

Part 2: Poets Speak

Introduction: *The Birth of Poems* – David Sutton   81
How Does a Poem Come About? (Years 9-12) – Roslyn Arnold   82
    Birdsong / Sunday Afternoon – Pittwater
The Art of Light Verse (Years 8-12) – Tim Hopkins   86
    Parkbenchers / Consequences / Cat / Elementary / Who
Remembering Childhood (Years 10-12) – Carl Leggo   88
    (With Suggested Activities by Glenys Acland & Joe Belanger)
    Growing Up Perpendicular on the Side of a Hill

Part 3: Some Additional Poetry Units

Playing With Language (Years 7-11) – Ken Watson   94
    Beheadings – Miroslav Holub
    A Group of Riddles
    Secret Message – Tim Hopkins
    Shakespeare – Tim Hopkins
    Elusive – Tim Hopkins
    Hiawatha – Henry Wadsworth Longfellow (excerpt)
    The Modern Hiawatha – George A Strong
    Coochi-Coochi – Bill Greenwell
    Sonnet in the Words of Shakespeare – Alison Pryde
What is a Poem? (Years 7-9) – Glenys Acland & Joe Belanger   100
    Shadows – Gary Boswell
    Hockey Player – Michael Nowlan
Changing the Point of View (Years 9-12) – Trevor Gambell & Sam Robinson   102
    The Doctor – Gary Hyland
Teaching *The Forsaken* (Years 10-12) – Joe Belanger   103
    The Forsaken – Duncan Campbell Scott
The Ballad Tradition (Years 7-10) – Glenys Acland, Joe Belanger, Ken Watson   107
    The Australian Ballad Tradition:
    The Death of Ben Hall – Anon
    How the Fire Queen Crossed the Swamp – Will Ogilvie
    The Ballad of Percival Pig – Kel Richards
    Two Canadian Ballads:
    The Squad of One – Robert Stead
    The Cremation of Sam McGee – Robert Service
Answers and Imitations: Exploring Tone (Years 10-12) – Ken Watson   119
    To Lucasta, Going to the Warres – Richard Lovelace
    To Lucasta: On Seeing No Hope of Returning From the Wars – John Manifold
    To Lucasta On Going to the Wars – For the Fourth Time – Robert Graves
    Alibi – Arthur Guiterman
Life Matters (Years 10-12) – Roslyn Arnold   124
    Yours Sincerely – Barry Cole
    Lending Library – David King
    How's That? – Norman Nicholson

Acknowledgements

Douglas Adams: Excerpt from *The Hitchhiker's Guide to the Galaxy* © Completely Unexpected Productions Ltd, reprinted by permission of the publishers, Pan Macmillan, London.

Ethel Anderson: *The Young Jackaroo* from **Squatter's Luck and Other Poems** by permission of Melbourne University Press.

Jeannette Armstrong: *History Lesson* from **Breathtracks** by Jeannette Armstrong (Theytus Books) by permission of the author.

Roslyn Arnold: *Sunday Afternoon – Pittwater* from **Mirror the Wind** by Roslyn Arnold (Sydney:St Clair Press, 1997), and *Birdsong*.

Raymond Carver: *Late Fragment* from **New Pathway to the Waterfall** (Collins Harvill, 1990) c Raymond Carver, 1990, reprinted by permission of International Creative Management Inc.

Barry Cole: *Yours Sincerely*, from **Inside Outside** (Shoestring Press, 1997), by permission of the author.

Catherine Fisher: *Words*, from **The Unexplored Ocean** (Seren Books, 1994) by permission of the publisher.

Robert Graves: *To Lucasta on Going to the Wars – for the Fourth Time*, from **Complete Poems Vol 1** (Carcanet, 1995) by permission of Carcanet Press.

Bill Greenwell: *Coochi-Coochi* by permission of the author.

John Heath-Stubbs: *History of the Flood*, from **Collected Poems 1943-87** by John Heath-Stubbs (Carcanet, 1988) by permission of David Higham Associates.

A D Hope: *Lucasta's Reply to Mr Richard Lovelace* by A D Hope, from his **A Book of Answers** (A & R, 1978) by permission of Curtis Brown (Aust) Pty Ltd.

Tim Hopkins: *Who, Parkbenchers, Consequences, Elementary, Cat, Secret Message, Shakespeare, Elusive* by permission of the author.

Robert Hull: *Columbus*, from **Encouraging Shakespeare** by Robert Hull (Peterloo Poets, 1993) by permission of the publisher.

Gary Hyland: *The Doctor*, by permission of the publishers, Thistledown Press

David King: *Lending Library* by permission of the author.

Carl Leggo: *Growing up Perpendicular on the Side of a Hill* by permission of the author; first published by Killick Press, St John's, Newfoundland.

Rhona McAdam: *White Dresses*, by permission of Thistledown Press.

F T Macartney: *Didjeridoo* and *Bargain Basement*, from **Selected Poems** by Frederick T Macartney (A & R) by permission of HarperCollins Publishers.

John Manifold: *To Lucasta: on seeing no immediate hope of returning from the wars*, from **Collected Verse** by John Manifold (1978), by permission of the University of Queensland Press.

Adrian Mitchell: *The Apeman Recollects Emotions in Tranquillity* from **The Apeman Cometh** (Cape 1975) © Adrian Mitchell, reprinted by permission of PFD on behalf of Adrian Mitchell. Educational Health Warning: Adrian Mitchell asks that none of his poems are used in connection with any examination whatsoever.

John Mole: *The Mobile Rag*, from **For the Moment** by John Mole (Peterloo Poets, 2000) by permission of the publisher.

Michael Nowlan: *Hockey Player*, by permission of the author.

Will Ogilvie: *How the Fire Queen Crossed the Swamp*, from **Fair Girls and Grey Horses** by Will Ogilvie (A. & R., 1926), by permission of Harper Collins Publishers.

Alison Pryde: *Sonnet in the Words of Shakespeare* from **Have We Had Easter Yet?** by Alison Pryde (Peterloo Poets, 1998) by permission of the publisher.

Kel Richards: *The Ballad of Percival Pig* from **Domestic Bliss and other Verse** by Kel Richards (Macmillan, 1988) by permission of the author.

William Scammell: *Junior Coaching*, from **The Game** by William Scammell (Peterloo Poets, 1992) by permission of the publisher.

Robert Service: *The Cremation of Sam McGee*, by permission of the estate of Robert W. Service.

Jon Stallworthy: *The Trap*, from **Rounding the Horn: Collected Poems** (Carcanet, 1998, by permission of the author.

Robert Stead: *The Squad of One*, by permission of the estate of Robert James Campbell Stead.

David Sutton: *The Birth of Poems*, from **A Holding Action** by David Sutton (Peterloo Poets, 2000) by permission of the publisher.

Colin Thiele: *Portraits*, from **Selected Verse** by Colin Thiele (Rigby, 1970) by permission of the author.

Harry Thurston: *Black Hull* by permission of the author.

Barrie Wade: Riddle from **My First Is in Monkey** (Collins Educational, 1996), by permission of the author.

Andrew Wreggitt: *At the Wedding* , by permission of Thistledown Press.

Kit Wright: *Song of the Whale* by permission of the author.

At the time of publication we have been unable to locate the copyright holders of the following poems, and would appreciate any assistance that readers may be able to give: *Green Beret* (Ho Thien), *Shadows* (Gary Boswell), *How's That?* (Norman Nicholson). *The Modern Hiawatha* (George Strong), *Alibi* (Arthur Guiterman). We have also been unable to contact the publishers of the English translations of the Li Bai poem.

Words

Catherine Fisher

They are stones
shaped to the hand.
Fling them accurately.

They are horses.
Bridle them;
they'll run away with you.

They are windows,
opening on vistas
that are unreachable.

They are apples.
Bite on hardness
to the sweet core.

They are coracles;
flimsy,
soon overloaded.

They are candles.
Carry them carefully.
They have burned cities.

(This poem is not part of a photocopiable unit.)

Part 1:
My Best
Poetry Unit

TEACHER'S PAGE

Performance Poetry in the Junior and Middle Secondary Years

Jean Hayhoe, Rachel Mapes, Ken Watson

The History of the Flood (Years 7-8)

This is an excellent poem for whole-class activity: Choral speaking/Performance. The skills involved are comprehension, memory, confidence-building, diction, dramatic presentation, voice projection, eye-contact skill, deportment and presence (Performance), group work, co-operation, cueing.

1. Teacher reads poem to class and they discuss what it seems to be about.

2. Introduce the idea of performing the poem as a class to a real audience (end-of-term entertainment etc. Make it a real audience!)

3. Allocate sections of the poem to individuals, pairs, groups or whole.

4. Give each child a copy of the scripted poem and ask them to highlight in one colour their individual parts and in another colour their group and the class parts.

5. As far as possible, they should learn their individual parts for homework. (As far as we are concerned they can use the script but have to be trained how to hold it when performing!)

6. Practise in class, sitting first, then standing as they would in front of an audience.

7. Practise in larger space (hall etc) for voice projection, stance, etc.

More Performance Poetry

The Apeman (Years 7-8)

The full title of this poem, which comes from a sequence of poems by Adrian Mitchell entitled *The Apeman Cometh*, is *The Apeman recollects emotions in tranquillity with a copy of the TLS stuck up his arse*. We have taken the liberty of giving it a shorter title, as the Wordsworthian reference would be lost on young students and the reference to the *Times Literary Supplement* would appear to be some sort of private joke.

The poem is ideal for whole-class use in Years 7 and 8. After a reading by the teacher, the poem could be placed on overhead and suggestions made by the students about how the class performance could be constructed (eg, deciding the best place(s) for whole-class chorus work, and where to get variety by using groups of three or four voices, or even a single voice). After that, twenty minutes of practice will produce a reading that will delight the class.

The next poem in the sequence, *Apeman as Tourist Guide*, begins:
>Apeman show you round jungle?
>All right.

If you don't feel it does violence to Mitchell's intentions, these two lines could be used as an introduction to the poem – the first line spoken by a single voice, with the whole class replying.

The Daniel Jazz (Years 7-8)

This poem is ideal for whole-class presentation. Let the kids decide how the poem should be presented.

The Young Jackaroo (Years 7-9)

A different group can take each stanza and prepare it for presentation. The refrain
>'Hup! Knickerbockerbuckaroo!

is chanted by the whole class.

Didjeridoo (Years 8-10)

Here the whole class can join in the haunting refrain, with different groups for each stanza. Or the poem can be presented as readers' theatre (see below).

Readers' Theatre (Years 9-11)

The oral side of poetry is often neglected in the middle and upper secondary years, perhaps because adolescents who have not been lucky enough to experience the joys of choral speaking in the upper primary and junior secondary years tend to react against it when teachers try to get their involvement in Years 9 and 10. For such students readers' theatre is the ideal way of restoring the oral dimension to poetry. Small groups (usually containing from four to seven or eight students) take up to twenty minutes or so to decide how a particular poem can be presented to the class. (Remind them that some lines of phrases might be said by the whole group, some by two voices, some by a single voice etc.) They also need to decide questions of tone and emphasis. After a couple of practice runs they can provide a book-in-hand reading that brings out their interpretation of the poem.

In addition to the poems in this section, Keats' *La Belle Dame Sans Merci* (p 49), Robert Hull's *Columbus* (p 63), and Norman Nicholson's *How's that?* (p 126) lend themselves to readers' theatre treatment, as do the ballads in the unit 'The Ballad Tradition'.

With extra preparation time, a musical background and sound effects can be produced. For example there are several CDs which feature the sound of whales 'singing'; one of these would provide a fine background to a presentation of Kit Wright's *The Song of the Whale*.

Performance Poetry, Junior & Middle Secondary Years

The History of the Flood

John Heath-Stubbs

Bang Bang Bang
Said the nails in the Ark.

It's getting rather dark
Said the nails in the Ark.

For the rain is coming down
Said the nails in the Ark.

And you're all like to drown
Said the nails in the Ark.

Dark and black as sin
Said the nails in the Ark.

So won't you all come in
Said the nails in the Ark.

But only two by two
Said the nails in the Ark.

So they came in two by two,
The elephant, the kangaroo,
And the gnu,
And the little tiny shrew.

Then the birds
Flocked in like wingéd words:
Two racket-tailed motmots, two macaws,
Two nuthatches and two
Little bright robins.

And the reptiles: the gila monster, the slow-worm,
The green mamba, the cottonmouth and the alligator —
All squirmed in;
And after a very lengthy walk,
Two giant Galapagos tortoises.

And the insects in their hierarchies:
A queen ant, a king ant, a queen wasp, a king wasp,
A queen bee, a king bee,
And all the beetles, bugs, and mosquitoes,
Cascaded in like glittering, murmurous jewels.

But the fish had their wish;
For the rain came down.
People began to drown:
The wicked, the rich —
They gasped out bubbles of pure gold,
Which exhalations
Rose to the constellations.

So for forty days and forty nights
They were on the waste of waters
In those cramped quarters.
It was very dark, damp and lonely.
There was nothing to see, but only
The rain which continued to drop.
It did not stop.

So Noah sent forth a Raven. The raven said 'Kark!
I will not go back to the Ark.'
The raven was footloose,
He fed on the bodies of the rich —
Rich with vitamins and goo.
They had become bloated,
And everywhere they floated.
The raven's heart was black,
He did not come back.
It was not a nice thing to do:

Which is why the raven is a token of wrath,
And creaks like a rusty gate
When he crosses your path; and Fate
Will grant you no luck that day:
The raven is fey:
You were meant to have a scare.
Fortunately in England
The raven is rather rare.

Then Noah sent forth a dove
She did not want to rove.
She longed for her love —
The other turtle dove —
(For her no other dove!)
She brought back a twig from an olive-tree.
There is no more beautiful tree
Anywhere on the earth,
Even when it comes to birth
From six weeks under the sea.

She did not want to rove.
She wanted to take her rest,
And to build herself a nest
All in the olive grove.
She wanted to make love.
She thought that was the best.

The dove was not a rover;
So they knew that the rain was over.
Noah and his wife got out
(They had become rather stout)
And Japhet, Ham, and Shem.
(The same could be said of them.)
They looked up at the sky.
The earth was becoming dry.

Then the animals came ashore :—
There were more of them than before:
There were two dogs and a litter of puppies;
There were a tom-cat and two tib-cats
And two litters of kittens — cats
Do not obey regulations;
And, as you might expect,
A quantity of rabbits.

God put a rainbow in the sky.
They wondered what it was for.
There had never been a rainbow before.
The rainbow was a sign;
It looked like a neon sign —
Seven colours arched in the skies:
What should it publicise?
They looked up with wondering eyes.
It advertises Mercy
Said the nails in the Ark.

Mercy Mercy Mercy.
Said the nails in the Ark.

Our God is merciful
Said the nails in the Ark.

Merciful and gracious
Bang Bang Bang Bang.

The Apeman

Adrian Mitchell

Jump that jungle
Jump that jungle
Pump that jungle
Pump that jungle
Eat that jungle
Eat that jungle
Heat that jungle
Heat that jungle
Joke that jungle
Joke that jungle
Soak that jungle
Soak that jungle
Sling that jungle
Sling that jungle
Sing that jungle
Sing that jungle
Grow that jungle
Grow that jungle
Blow that jungle
Blow that jungle
Make that jungle
Make that jungle
Shake that jungle
Shake that jungle
Climb that jungle
Climb that jungle
Chime that jungle
Chime that jungle
Plumb that jungle
Plumb that jungle
Come that jungle
Come that jungle
Shove that jungle
Shove that jungle
Love that jungle
Love that jungle
The jungle loves you.

The Daniel Jazz

Vachel Lindsay

Darius the Mede was a king and a wonder.
His eye was proud, and his voice was thunder.
He kept bad lions in a monstrous den.
He fed up the lions on Christian men.

Daniel was the chief hired man of the land.
He stirred up the music in the palace band.
He whitewashed the cellar. He shovelled in the coal.
And Daniel kept-a-praying: "Lord save my soul."
Daniel kept-a-praying: "Lord save my soul."
Daniel kept-a-praying: "Lord save my soul."

Daniel was the butler, swagger and swell.
He ran up stairs. He answered the bell.
And he would let in whoever came a-calling:
Saints so holy, scamps so appalling.
"Old man Ahab leaves his card.
Elisha and the bears are a-waiting in the yard.
Here comes Pharaoh and his snakes a-calling.
Here comes Cain and his wife a-calling.
Shadrach, Meshach and Abednego for tea.
Here comes Jonah and the whale,
And the Sea!
Here comes St Peter and his fishing pole.
Here comes Judas and his silver a-calling.
Here comes old Beelzebub a-calling."
And Daniel kept-a-praying: "Lord save my soul."
Daniel kept-a-praying: "Lord save my soul."
Daniel kept-a-praying: "Lord save my soul."

His sweetheart and his mother were Christian and meek.
They washed and ironed for Darius every week.
One Thursday he met them at the door:
Paid them as usual, but acted sore.
He said: "Your Daniel is a dead little pigeon.
He's a good hard worker, but he talks religion."
And he showed them Daniel in the lion's cage.
Daniel standing quietly, the lions in a rage.
His good old mother cried:
"Lord save him."
And Daniel's tender sweetheart cried:
"Lord save him."

And she was a golden lily in the dew.
And she was as sweet as an apple on the tree.
And she was as fine as a melon in the cornfield.
Gliding and lovely as a ship on the sea,
Gliding and lovely as a ship on the sea.

And she prayed to the Lord:
"Send Gabriel. Send Gabriel."

King Darius said to the lions:
"Bite Daniel. Bite Daniel.
Bite him. Bite him. Bite him!"

Thus roared the lions: -
"We want Daniel, Daniel, Daniel,
We want Daniel, Daniel, Daniel.
Grrrrrrrrrrrrrrrrrrrrrrrrrrrrrrrrrr
Grrrrrrrrrrrrrrrrrrrrrrrrrrrrrrrrrrr"

And Daniel did not frown.
Daniel did not cry.
He kept on looking at the sky.
And the Lord said to Gabriel:
"Go chain the lions down,
Go chain the lions down,
Go chain the lions down,
Go chain the lions down."

And Gabriel chained the lions,
And Gabriel chained the lions,
And Gabriel chained the lions.
And Daniel got out of the den,
And Daniel got out of the den,
And Daniel got out of the den.
And Darius said: "You're a Christian child."
Darius said: "You're a Christian child."
Darius said: "You're a Christian child."
And gave him his job again,
And gave him his job again,
And gave him his job again.

The Young Jackaroo

Ethel Anderson

Jack Brady tit-tit-tup-ped once into Bourke,
On his thoroughbred stallion he soon set to work
To give a display
In a negligent way
Of what a good buckjumping rider could do.
(Hup! Knickerbockerbuckaroo!)

For forty-six seconds in every man's sight
Jack Brady on Boomerang's saddle sat tight,
While singular curves
Swift convulsions and swerves
Showed what a good buckjumping waler could do.
(Hup! Knickerbockerbuckaroo!)

Then out spoke a jackaroo newly come west,
"Your beast is a beauty, but mine is the best,
His name is well known
From Gilgandra to Scone,

As the king bucking brumby this side the Barcoo."
(Hup! Knickerbockerbuckaroo!)

For sixty true seconds he held his head high
While the outlaw astonished the men standing by
With kangaroo-leaps
And miraculous peeps
Through his hooves at the back of the young jackaroo.
(Hup! Knickerbockerbuckaroo!)

Then an old-timer draped in a ten-gallon lid
Exclaimed, "That's the best that a man ever did!
He could gallop away
On Dan Dargan's mad grey!"
So they handed the stake to the young jackaroo!
(Hup! Knickerbockerbuckaroo!)

Didjeridoo

F C Macartney

Didjeridoo—didjeridoo!
A blackfellow blows through a length of bamboo
To the regular beat of an ironwood stick,
Click-click, click-click-click;
The throb of his breath is the ghost of a drum
With a madness of apathy muffling its thrum.
The sun, a red gasp, sinks down in its throes,
And the night waits for wind as a coward for blows;
And all that the world ever wanted or knew
Is dark while you hark to the didjeridoo.

Didjeridoo—didjeridoo!
A nursery rhyme and a history too.
Black faces lean over a flickering fire;
A nasal chant rises, drops low, rises higher,
Then wearily fades to an echo of wind
Over withering grasses that footsteps have thinned
Through nomadic ages, space without scope,
Unscarred by regret and unharassed by hope;
For primitive ages are distanced into
A groan to the bone by the didjeridoo.

Didjeridoo—didjeridoo!
Even the pastorals, lyric with dew,
Piped in Arcadian meadows, so green
And so golden and glad and so mythically clean,
Are not so remote as this shudder of sound,
Which broods like a beast nuzzling close to the ground
For the track of its mate or an answering wail.
This piper sits playing and knows all things fail.
The days are so many, the years are so few,
Says the thud, as of mud, in the didjeridoo.

The Song Of The Whale

Kit Wright

Heaving mountain in the sea,
Whale, I heard you
Grieving.

Great whale, crying for your life,
Crying for your kind, I knew
How we would use
Your dying:

Lipstick for our painted faces,
Polish for our shoes.

Tumbling mountain in the sea,
Whale, I heard you
Calling.

Bird-high notes, keening, soaring:
At their edge a tiny drum
Like a heartbeat.

We would make you
Dumb.

In the forest of the sea,
Whale, I heard you
Singing,

Singing to your own kind,
We'll never let you be.
Instead of life we choose

Lipstick for our painted faces,
Polish for our shoes.

Junior Coaching

William Scammell

Throw the ball up. Try to whack it
    over the net and in that square.
No no, Fiona! With the racquet!
    Tom, stop pulling Janet's hair.
Yes, Dave, racquets cost a packet.
    Oh, your dad's a millionaire.

That's all right then. What's his swindle?
    No, Tom, you can't smash just yet.
When you're tall and tough as Lendl . . .
    Darren, don't let down that net!
Now girls, who said you could spend all
    afternoon tormenting Brett?

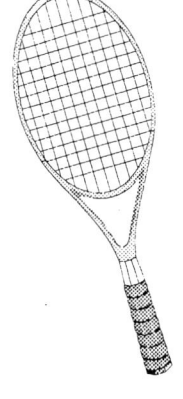

Watch the ball! Turn! Arm back early!
    Bend your knees, and follow through!
Just like this. Look. Oh, well nearly.
    Now let's see what you can do.
Well done, Kimberley! You've clearly
    volleyed that to Timbuctoo!

Dave, I think your track suit's smashing.
    Yes, I like the headband too.
You've got the gear, you've got the passion,
    just like teenage McEnroe.
Now hit the ball, and try to ration
    all the things your mouth can do.

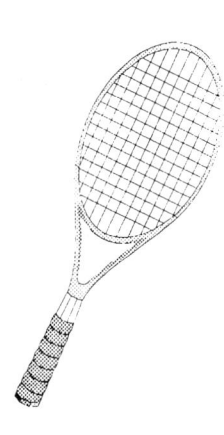

Pick up balls, please! Come on, quickly!
    Balls to me! Now who threw that?
Kimberley, you look quite sickly.
    What? You've lost your new school hat?
Thank you, Darren. Yes, it's triff'ckly
    tightly strung, your Becker bat.

Quiet! QUIET! Thanks a million.
    Got *all* your stuff? See you next week.
Kate, you may. In the pavilion.
    Well, there goes the nation's freak-
y, cheeky, whacky, billion brill ones
    piping homeward, in the peak!

The Mobile Rag

John Mole

Out of your pocket, up to your face,
any occasion, any old place,
dial those digits, watch this space
doing the mobile,
it's in the bag,
yes, doing the mobile rag.

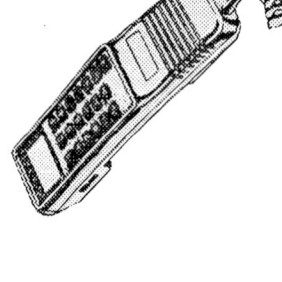

Chase your client, hurry that lunch,
bend your ear, let your shoulder hunch,
hear those Japanese numbers crunch
doing the mobile,
Porsch or Jag,
yes, doing the mobile rag.

Stride down the platform, turn on your heel,
swagger and strut from deal to deal,
small cogs know that you're the big wheel
doing the mobile,
light up a fag,
yes, doing the mobile rag.

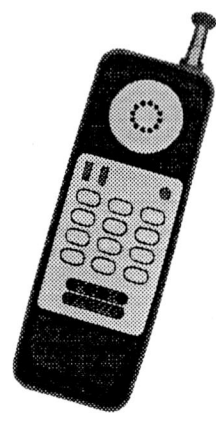

Put in the boot, sharpen the knife,
this is the action, this is the life,
always cut short the call from your wife
doing the mobile,
nag nag nag
doing the mobile rag.

Honour your partner? Keep your old car?
Who the hell do they think you are!
Look at that split skirt over by the bar
doing the mobile,
top shelf mag,
doing the mobile rag.

Wire up the e-mail, tighten the net,
shaft your department without regret,
there's room at the top and you'll make it yet
doing the mobile,
doing the mobile,
doing that mobile rag.

The Unquiet Grave

Anon

'The wind doth blow today, my love,
    And a few small drops of rain;
I never had but one true-love,
    In a cold grave she was lain.

'I'll do as much for my true-love
    As any young man may;
I'll sit and mourn all at her grave
    For a twelvemonth and a day.'

The twelvemonth and a day being up,
    The dead began to speak:
'Oh who sits weeping on my grave,
    And will not let me sleep?'

''Tis I, my love, sits on your grave,
    And will not let you sleep;
For I crave one kiss of your clay-cold lips,
    And that is all I seek.'

'You crave one kiss of my clay-cold lips;
    But my breath smells earthy strong;
If you have one kiss of my clay-cold lips,
    Your time will not be long.

''Tis down in yonder garden green,
    Love, where we used to walk,
The finest flower that ere was seen
    Is withered to a stalk.

'The stalk is withered dry, my love,
    So will our hearts decay;
So make yourself content, my love,
    Till God calls you away.'

Bargain Basement

F T Macartney

Not there, my dear, not there:
this way—down the stair.

Have you a line of hillocks and some white
absurd young lambs, all wool, and light
as leaping air?

No, sir—sorry! . . .
All right, don't worry.

You keep, perhaps,
some inexpensive scraps
of early green
springtime sateen,
with colour partly lost
in folds of frost,
prinked with those flowers that smell
so sweetly?—I know them well
but can't recall the name:
I saw them somewhere a month ago.

Unfortunately, madam, no. . . .
Ah, what a shame!

I say, I'd like a length of thin
pale sea-water to wear next to the skin.
None? A creek, then?—with embroideries
of eucalypt-trees,
the soldierly sort that gets
dignity from its golden epaulets.

No, sir, impossible. . . .
Oh, well—

Then do you stock
that delicate sort of frock
now worn by blossoming orchards, thin,
wide and airy, like a crinoline?

No, madam, no; but I might find. . . .
Oh, never mind.
Come on, my dear:
there's nothing for us here.
Thank goodness, we still have, in the Lay-by
(for what it's worth
when we two die)
that remnant double-width of damaged earth!

TEACHER'S PAGE

From Poem to Picture Book (Years 9-11) — John Douglas

The idea behind this unit is appropriate for Years 7 and 8 as well, but this poem is too sophisticated for junior secondary students. With an able Year 10 class:

1. I put the text of Margaret Barbalet's *The Wolf*, illustrated by Jane Tanner, (Viking 1991) on a series of overhead transparencies and read it to the students. I didn't say it was a picture book (though my surprise fizzled because many of them knew it already).

2. I reread the story in sections and asked them to tell me what they noticed. We discussed the fact that the father was absent from this family, that it was the oldest male child who first hears the wolf (taking the place of the father?), that there are repeated references to the security of the landscape as it used to be, and so on. The discussion wasn't conclusive – I don't see how it could be, but they had got the idea that their fear made the wolf more threatening and that to face and accept it was to find its power to frighten diminished. That was the bridge into *The Trap*.

3. Somewhere along the way we talked about the illustrations and the way in which they offered a kind of visual commentary upon and interpretation of this elusive and enigmatic text. I wanted them to use their illustrations to do exactly the same thing with *The Trap*.

4. I read *The Trap* from an overhead transparency and we discussed similarities and differences between what happens in *The Wolf* and in *The Trap*. The similarities are obvious and interesting e.g. the way the creature comes insistently closer and closer, the way in which the house takes on a symbolic value such that the breaching of the house in both texts is a decisive moment, the fact that fear makes the threat grow, the possibility that what is feared is not an external threat so much as something inside the individual (or, in the case of *The Wolf*, inside the family), the way in which lawn, wallflowers, etc. become symbols of nature tamed and the wolf seems more and more to represent something that is untamed, savage, uncivilised or uncivilisable.

5. The students formed working groups of 4 or 5. Their job was to divide the text up in such a way that it would accompany a maximum of six pictures and to turn *The Trap* into a picture book for adolescents or adults. The pictures had to be interpretative, not merely illustrative, and the completed picture book was to form the basis of a group oral presentation.

6. Most of the exploration of the poem took place in the small groups. At first many of the students had difficulty thinking of the wolf as a symbol for something inside the man that he cannot face or accept and which grows more powerful the more he attempts to destroy it. (I gave them a handout about the Jungian concept of 'the shadow', not as an answer to the identity of the monster but as offering perhaps a way of beginning to talk about what it is inside the man that the monster represents.) However, all the students finally came up with an account of the poem that dealt with this central idea adequately.

7. The drawings were to be done in black lead pencil (no point wasting lesson after lesson in producing full-colour art works) and in any case the oral presentation was where they could elaborate on what they imagined the pictures might have looked like if taken to their fullest point of development.

8. Some of their work was extraordinary. One group, for instance, in the drawing that accompanied the section about the man setting his engine in his porch, drew the trap with gaping jaws like the wolf's mouth, but the rest of the trap was the man's body, showing that he was both what he feared and the author of his own destruction.

9. I also videotaped all the group oral presentations.

10. It was hugely successful: (a) as a way of encouraging sustained attention to and reflection on a complex text (b) as a way of generating a sustained small group activity (c) as a way of leading up to a sustained oral presentation on a text (some of them went for twenty minutes). The disadvantage was that we heard 8 presentations on the same poem. If I could have found another text the equal of Stallworthy's, then maybe we could have had four presentations on each text. However, the presentations were so different that the students' interest was held.

From Poem to Picture Book

The Trap

Jon Stallworthy

The first night that the monster lurched
Out of the forest on all fours,
He saw its shadow in his dream
Circle the house, as though it searched
For one it loved or hated. Claws
On gravel and a rabbit's scream
Ripped the fabric of his dream.

Waking between dark and dawn
And sodden sheets, his reason quelled
The shadow and the nightmare sound.
The second night it crossed the lawn
A brute voice in the darkness yelled.
He struggled up, woke raving, found
His wall-flowers trampled to the ground.

When rook wings beckoned the shadows back
He took his rifle down, and stood
All night against the leaded glass.
The moon ticked round. He saw the black
Elm-skeletons in the doomsday wood,
The sailing and the failing stars
And red coals dropping between bars.

The third night such a putrid breath
Fouled, flared his nostrils, that he turned,
Turned, but could not lift, his head.
A coverlet as thick as death
Oppressed him: he crawled out: discerned
Across the door his watchdog, dead.
'Build a trap,' the neighbours said.

All that day he built his trap
With metal jaws and a spring as thick
As the neck of a man. One touch
Triggered the hanging teeth: jump, snap,
And lightning guillotined the stick
Thrust in its throat. With gun and torch
He set his engine in the porch.

The fourth night in their beds appalled
His neighbours heard the hunting roar
Mount, mount to an exultant shriek.
At daybreak timidly they called
His name, climbed through the splintered door,
And found him sprawling in the wreck,
Naked, with a severed neck.

TEACHER'S PAGE

The Editorial Committee (Years 8-11) — Ken Watson

What was without doubt my most successful poetry lesson has already been published – in *Jigsaw* (St Clair Press, 1995), the predecessor of this volume. It involved the presentation of a difficult poem, *plato told* by e e cummings, followed by having the students, in groups, compiling questions about the poem to which they really wanted to know the answers. These questions were then blackboarded for the class as a whole to consider. This is a procedure which works well with a range of poetry for Year 9 and above. But since I can't repeat that unit I offer the "editorial committee" approach, which has worked well for me in a number of contexts.

Here is another situation in which the editorial committee idea has proved successful. Year 8 students (ie, aged 13-14) were reading Hans Peter Richter's novel *Friedrich*, which deals with the tragedy of a Jewish boy in Germany before and during World War II. As a final activity, the students, in groups, were given copies of half a dozen poems from *I Never Saw Another Butterfly* (NY: Schocken Books, 1978), a collection of poems written by children in the Terezin Concentration Camp near Prague between 1942 and 1944, together with some photographs from the Nazi period. Each group was then asked to imagine itself an editorial committee from a publishing house preparing a deluxe edition of *Friedrich*. The committee would determine which photographs would be appropriate to include, which poem could appear as an epigraph, and which poem could appear at the end of the novel. The groups then had to justify their choices to the rest of the class. I am sure that this activity would work well with novels in the higher grades for which a group of appropriate poems can be gathered together. The task of finding such poems is made easier by referring to the most recent edition of *Where's That Poem?* by Helen Morris (Hemel Hempstead: Simon & Schuster).

The Golden Vanity

This ballad dates from the early seventeenth century. Three versions are offered here, but the teacher may wish to exclude the third, which differs so markedly from the other two. The task is within the range of able Year 7s, but it probably works best at about Year 9 level. I do strongly recommend that the students hear at least one good reading (ideally by the teacher), and then read the ballads over silently to themselves, before forming into editorial committees.

The Three Ravens/The Twa Corbies

The old Scottish ballads, *The Three Ravens* and *The Twa Corbies*, are clearly related, though in some respects they are the opposite of each other.

The first version of *The Twa Corbies* is the earlier one; the second is more elaborate and more self-consciously literary.

Particularly if the class has considered four or more of the ballads, groups could be invited to compose a definition of the literary term "ballad" as it applies to these traditional verses.

STUDENTS' PAGE

The Editorial Committee (1)

You and your group are members of an editorial committee assembled by a publishing company to put together a collection of old English and Scottish ballads. The problem is that in some cases there are several versions of the same ballad; your task is to decide which version is that one that should appear in the book. You will need to give reasons for your choice to the publishing company (the rest of the class).

1: The Golden Vanity

Oh there was a lofty ship and a lofty ship was she
And the name of that ship was the Golden Vanity
And they feared she would be taken by the Turkish Enemy
As she sailed on the lowland, lowland low
As she sailed on the lowland sea

Up stepped a little cabin boy, a cabin boy was he
And he said to the Captain what will you give to me
If I sneak alongside the Turkish Enemy
And I sink her in the lowland, lowland low
And I sink her in the lowland sea

Oh I will give you silver and I will give you gold
And the hand of my daughter your bonnie bride will be
If you'll sneak alongside of the Turkish Enemy
And you'll sink her in the lowland lowland low
And you'll sink her in the lowland sea

So he jumped overboard and overboard jumped he
And he swam alongside of the Turkish Enemy
And with a little drilling tool he boréd holes three
And he sank her in the lowland lowland low
He sank her in the lowland sea

Then he turned himself around and back again swam he
'Til he came to the side of the Golden Vanity
But the captain would not heed, for his daughter he did need
And he left him in the lowland lowland low
He left him in the lowland sea

Well his shipmates brought him out, but upon the deck he died
And they wrapped him in his blanket that was so soft and wide
And they cast him overboard and he drifted with the tide
And he sank beneath the lowland lowland low
He sank beneath the lowland sea

2: The Golden Vanity

Oh there was a ship that sailed, all across the lowland sea
And the name of the ship was the Golden Vanity
And we feared she would be taken by the Spanish enemy
And they'd sink her in the lowland, lo
They'd sink her in the lowland sea.

Then boldly up spoke our little cabin boy,
Saying: "What would you give me if the galley I destroy?
If I sink her in the lowland, lowland low,
If I sink her in the lowland sea."

"A treasure chest of gold and silver I'll give to thee
And my own fairest daughter, thy bonnie bride shall be
If you'll swim along side the Spanish enemy
And sink her in the lowland, lowland low
If you'll sink her in the lowland sea."

So, the boy he made ready, and overboard sprang he,
And he swam to the side of the Spanish enemy
And with his brace and auger, in her side he bored holes three
And sank her in the lowland, lowland lo
He sank her in the lowland sea.

Then the boy, he did swim back, to the cheering of the crew
But the captain would not heed him, for his promise he did rue
He scorned his sad entreaties, though loudly he did sue
And he left him in the lowland, lowland lo
He left him in the lowland sea.

Then the boy he turned round and swam to the port side
And up unto his messmates, full bitterly he cried,
Saying "Messmates, pull me up for I'm drifting with the tide,
And I'm sinking in the lowland, lowland low
I'm sinking in the lowland sea."

Well his messmates pulled him up but on the deck he died
And they placed him in his hammock, which was so fair and wide,
And they lowered him down, and over the port side
And he sank into the lowland, lo
He sank into the lowland sea.

My Best Poetry Unit

3: The Golden Vanity

A ship called *The Golden Vanity*
Saw a Turkish man-of-war at sea.

The ship-boy spoke, "Captain," said he,
"If I sink her, what will you give to me?"

The captain replied, "You're brave and bold,
I'll give you a box of silver and gold."

"Then tie me tight in a black bull's skin,
And throw me in the sea, to sink or swim!"

They tied him tight in a black bull's skin
And threw him in the sea, to sink or swim.

The water was cold, but he kept afloat,
And away he swam to the Turkish boat.

Some were playing cards and some throwing dice,
When he made three holes in the boat with his knife.

He made three more....Then – lose or win –
What did it matter when the sea rushed in?

Some cut their coats, come cut their caps
To try to stop the salt water gaps.

About and about and about swam he,
And back to *The Golden Vanity*.

"Now throw me a rope and pull me on board!
Captain, see that you keep your word!"

"I'll throw you no rope," the captain cried,
"Goodbye, I leave you to drift with the tide."

Out spoke the ship-boy, out spoke he,
"What if I sink you? How would that be?"

"Throw him a rope!" the sailors cried,
They threw him a rope – but on deck he died.

The Editorial Committee (2)

You and your group are members of an editorial committee assembled by a publishing company to put together a collection of old English and Scottish ballads. The problem is that in some cases there are several versions of the same ballad; your task is to decide which version is the one that should appear in the book. You will need to give reasons for your choice to the publishing company (the rest of the class).

Two versions of a Scottish ballad:

The Twa Corbies

As I was walking all alane,
I heard twa corbies making a mane;
The tane unto the t'other say,
"Where sall we gang and dine to-day?"

"In behint yon auld fail dyke,
I wot there lies a new slain knight;
And naebody kens that he lies there,
But his hawk, his hound, and lady fair.

"His hound is to the hunting gane,
His hawk to fetch the wild-fowl hame,
His lady's ta'en another mate,
So we may mak our dinner sweet.

"Ye'll sit on his white hause-bane,
And I'll pike out his bonny blue een;
Wi' ae lock o' his gowden hair
We'll theek our nest when it grows bare.

"Mony a one for him makes mane,
But nane sall ken where he is gane;
O'er his white banes, when they be bare,
The wind sall blaw for evermair."

twa = two
corbies = crows (or ravens)
fail dyke = wall of turf
wot = know
kens = knows
hause-bane = neck bone
een = eye
theek = thatch

Two Ravens

There were two ravens sat on a tree,
Large and black as black may be,
And one unto the other gan say,
"Where shall we go and dine today?
Shall we go dine by the wild salt sea?
Shall we go dine 'neath the greenwood tree?

"As I sat on the deep sea sand,
I saw a fair ship nigh at land;
I waved my wings, I bent my beak,
The ship sank, and I heard a shriek:
There lie the sailors, one, two, three;
I shall dine by the wild salt sea."

"Come, I will show ye a sweeter sight,
A lonesome glen and a new-slain knight;
His bleed yet on the grass is hot,
His sword half drawn, his shafts unshot,
And no one kens that he lies there,
But his hawk, his hound, and his lady fair.

"His hound is to the hunting gane,
His hawk to fetch the wild fowl hame,
His lady's away with another mate,
So we shall make our dinner sweet;
Our dinner's sure, our feasting free,
Come, and dine by the greenwood tree.

"Ye shall sit on his white hause-bane,
I will pick out his bonny blue een;
Ye'll take a tress of his yellow hair,
To theak yere nest when it grows bare;
The gowden down on his young chin
Will do to rowe my young ones in.

"O, cauld and bare will his bed be
When winter storms sing in the tree;
At his head a tuft, at his feet a stone,
He will sleep, nor hear the maidens moan;
O'er his white bones the birds shall fly,
The wild deer bound and foxes cry."

When your group has studied the two versions, made your choice and assembled your arguments for presentation to the class, you could look at the following ballad, which is clearly related to the previous two. What similarities do you find? What are the differences? If you could include only one of the three in the proposed collection, would you consider *The Three Ravens*? Why, or why not?

The Three Ravens

There were three ravens sat on a tree,
They were as black as they might be.

The one of them said to his make,
"Where shall we our breakfast take?"

"Down in yonder greene field
There lies a knight slain under his shield;

"His hounds they lie down at his feet,
So well they can their master keep:

"His hawks they flie so eagerly,
There's no fowl dare come him nigh."

Down there comes a fallow doe
As great with young as she might goe.

She lift up his bloudy head,
And kist his wounds that were so red.

She gat him up upon her back
And carried him to earthen lake.

She buried him before the prime,
She was dead herself ere evensong time.

God send every gentleman
Such hounds, such hawks, and such a leman.

make = mate
leman = lover

TEACHER'S PAGE

The Worst Poem in the Universe (Year 9-12)
Gordon Shrubb

This poetry lesson is guaranteed to inspire every student to write a poem because the task invites criticism, parody, and mockery of "serious" poetry. It tends to work best in Years 9 and 10. The concept of satire has begun to flourish like a well watered weed in the garden of each student's mind.

One of the ironies in this poetry lesson is that while each student is released to write "bad" poetry, there is no sanction against entertainment. So, many of these "worst" poems are often wildly hilarious, and may even be considered to be "good". In fact, the best "worst" poem will almost always make this paradoxical paradigm shift. Many occupy the realm of dead-pan black humour, or even bed-pan bleak humour. Others will out-endgame Beckett.

The stimulus material from *The Hitchhiker's Guide to the Galaxy* also helps to broaden the choice of subject matter for those students who say "I can't think of anything to write about". Science fiction, technology, space ships, star systems, zero gravity, light travel, aliens, odd words, being a prisoner, competitions, and even poetry classrooms themselves, all suddenly pop into student view.

The writing task will fit any normal lesson length. However, the performances of the poems can spill over into the next lesson. It is important to encourage students to think about how they will perform the finished product. There is a theatrical dimension to the presentation of each poem. Each student needs to work with a partner for at least one rehearsal to assess its effect on an audience. This is one of the bonuses of this poetry lesson. In fact, the whole task can be repeated two or three times during a school year without any loss of interest from the students.

Finally, as in most competitions, there is the notion of a "prize". I like the treats scattered to audiences in the drama improvisations called 'Theatre Sports'. So, at the end of the class performance I make sure everyone gets a "Mintie" or a "Chocolate Frog" for the best. This has usually been decided by a quick straw vote from the class.

(Note: Always keep a copy of the best "worst" poem. This eventual repertoire can inspire other decades of poetry classes not yet even born.)

STUDENTS' PAGE

Worst Poem in the Universe

Worst Poem in the Universe Competition
Inspired by Douglas Adams'
The Hitch Hiker's Guide to the Galaxy

'You want to know about Vogons, so I enter the name so.' His fingers tapped some more keys. 'And there we are.'

The words Vogon Constructor Fleets flared in green across the screen. Ford pressed a large red button at the bottom of the screen and words began to undulate across it. At the same time, the book began to speak the entry as well in a still quiet measured voice.

'Vogon Constructor Fleets. Here is what to do if you want to get a lift from a Vogon: forget it. They are one of the most unpleasant races in the Galaxy – not actually evil, but bad tempered, bureaucratic, officious and callous. They wouldn't even lift a finger to save their own grandmothers from the Ravenous Bugblatter Beast of Traal without orders signed in triplicate, sent in, sent back, queried, lost, found, subjected to public enquiry, lost again, and finally buried in soft peat for three months and recycled as firelighters. ... On no account allow a Vogon to read poetry at you.'

(Prostetnic Vogon Jeltz, the commander of the Vogon fleet, captures Arthur and Ford.)

Arthur and Ford sat in Poetry Appreciation chairs – strapped in. Vogons suffered no illusions as to the regard their literary works were generally held in.

The sweat stood out cold on Ford Prefect's brow, and slid round the electrodes strapped to his temples. These were attached to a battery of electronic equipment – imagery intensifiers, rhythmic modulators, alliterative residulators, and simile dumpers – all designed to heighten the experience of the poem and make sure that not a single nuance of the poet's thought was lost.

Arthur Dent sat and shivered. He knew that he hadn't liked anything that had happened so far and didn't think that things were likely to change. Prostetnic Vogon Jeltz began to read.

Task

❖ Write the worst poem you can think of.

❖ Let your imagination begin to disintegrate as limply as an old perished rubber band.

My Best Poetry Unit

TEACHER'S PAGE

The Poetry Detective (Years 11-12) — Matthew Brown

An Introductory Exercise

Give the students copies of unnamed and untitled poems (excerpts would be sufficient) covering a range of historical periods. Begin with Chaucer and move through to at least one late twentieth century poet.

- ❖ Have the students work in small groups to place the poems in a chronological order. Each group would need to be able to justify their order. References to poetic language, style and/or themes would be most useful.

Repeat this exercise using only twentieth century poets from a range of cultures. Ensure that there are some women and Australian poets represented in your selection.

- ❖ Which poems were written by women? Be prepared to justify your decisions.
- ❖ Is it possible to determine the cultural influence of the poetry? Which cultures? Be prepared to justify your decisions.

The Unit

The Poetry Detective may be best utilised with a class which has either examined one or more of the Romantic poets or perhaps studied this period of literature or history. However, if your class successfully completed the introductory exercise, the students may have a sufficient awareness of the historical period making further study unnecessary at this time.

You may wish to introduce one or more of the Romantic poets to your class and have the students work on this unit as an extension exercise complementing their study. It may be more appropriate to use this activity as an extension for one or more students. It may also be completed by small groups of students to develop their research skills.

Consider having the students respond to this exercise as a narrative, both explaining and describing the research that they completed to resolve the mysteries of the chest. You may choose to give clues to the period or authorship to hasten the completion time required for the activities. The names referred to at various times through the unit of work include: Joseph Severn, John Keats, Percy Bysshe Shelley, Leigh Hunt and William Hazlitt.

Footnote References

1. (p30) The last lines of this document are attributed to Keats in a final letter written by him in Italy in 1821.
2. (p30) *Adonais*, Percy Bysshe Shelley. A poem written by Shelley on Keats's death.
3. (p31) "He [Keats] wrote this untitled eight-line fragment ... These were probably the last serious lines of poetry Keats wrote." Hirsch, Edward *How to Read a Poem* Harcourt, 1999.
4. (p31) An excerpt from *On Sitting Down to Read King Lear Again* (lines 6-14). A full copy of this poem is an effective complement to a study of **King Lear**.
5. (p32) Keats in a letter to Richard Woodhouse, 27 October 1818. Hirsch, Edward *How to Read a Poem*, p131.
6. (p32) *Bright Star* is believed to be Keats's last poem, perhaps begun in 1819 and completed in September 1820 when he copied it into Severn's copy of Shakespeare's poems during his voyage to Italy.
7. (p33) Keats in a letter to Benjamin Bailey - 22 November 1817. Haskell, D, *The Poetry of John Keats* (1991) p8.

The Poetry Detective

The task before you is to unravel the mysteries of the content of the chest. The texts that emerge are the work of published writers. Many of the excerpts provided are either wholly genuine or adaptations of original work.

You will find it most useful to imagine yourself in the role of the narrator. The answers to the questions will help to lead you to discover the authorship and a deeper understanding of the texts. You will develop a clearer understanding of the poets and poetry if you unravel the contents of the chest in the order that they are presented to you. There are questions asked of several of the excerpts that may be best answered by completing the research that is either recommended or implied as necessary. The most challenging questions are those requiring personal responses while making reference to the evidence provided by the chest.

The Chest

The small chest came into your possession along with a range of other items that had been auctioned as a lot from an English family estate with no surviving relatives. The firm responsible for the auction was only interested in quickly recouping their costs and did not take the trouble to examine the items carefully. An investment of interest, time and care on their part would have paid dividends – their loss, your reward.

You place the wooden coffer onto your work-table. Your first attempts to lift the lid had failed. You resolve to finish cleaning the outer shell of the chest before making another attempt to reveal its contents. You do not know how old it is nor how long it has been left unopened but its appearance suggests many, many years. You carefully brush and rub away at the dust and grime that has hidden the beauty of the rosewood which is gradually exposed with each moment of care you give to its restoration. The polishing oils seep into your hands and the quality of the finish is revealed to fingers made sensitive by the work of cleaning.

Now that the chest is clean you attempt to lift the lid again, carefully. On this occasion it opens with relative ease. Its first breath is shared with you. There is the scent of paper, very old paper, ink and a hint of time long past. Apparently it was never intended to hold a hidden fortune and you feel a touch of disappointment – there seems such a natural connection between chests, past ages and lost treasure.

The paper concertinas to fill the space where the lid had held the contents in place. You consider that the paper may be much younger than you had first thought – your first, and you hope your last, error. The top sheet that had folded out to you breaks away like a fine and fragile piece of ice as you place your hand on it. You determine not to make that mistake again. You discover the folded sheets of paper are equally brittle and you take great care to minimise further damage. Unfortunately a number of the sheets of paper have already broken along their folds, while others remain inexplicably whole. A bottle of ink had been left sealed inside the chest but history has long since dried its contents. A number of quills lie beside the dried ink on the bottom of the chest. Words and thoughts never to be written making those discovered all the more precious. You consider for a moment that there is more than one type of treasure. But what have you found?

STUDENTS' PAGE

A few letters and lines of verse ... poetry! You had continued to hope for wills, maps and other types of documents that might still promise wealth. Nonetheless, this is your chest and these are now your letters and poems. Curiosity captures you again.

The first page, broken along its folds, creates a simple puzzle. It is a part of letter ... perhaps the last page:

> *My Health has continued to deteriorate and my physician and friends recommend that I go to Italy. They believe a warmer winter may improve my humour. I am less optimistic as you know my family has had little good fortune in this regard. If this indeed is my last message to you I ask that you regard this Scrap of Paper to be my Last Will and Testament.*
>
> *My Chest of Books divide among my friends.*[1]

What is the mood of the author? There is a signature of sorts but it is entirely illegible. A surname of five or six letters which either time or the author's smudged carelessness has resulted in masked ownership.

It is an interesting line on which to finish a letter. Some of the poetry you have evidenced on the other pages may be the work of this letter's author. This seems a reasonable hypothesis given the contents of the chest.

You carefully examine the craftsmanship of the handwriting and you note clear consistency between some pages but you realise that there is more than one author represented here. One hand is precise, careful – you might even suggest purposeful and confident. Another is hesitant, perhaps afraid of the words that reveal segments of thought and emotion. And still a third style appears, tired, but the mind of the author is readily apparent.

You find that you are able to read parts of a letter written in another hand but like the first letter, it is incomplete and the author remains anonymous.

> *I shall miss his passion and his artist's eye. Joseph tells me that he remained interested in his work to the last having written the most extraordinary sonnet while on board ship. Joseph would have proven to be an excellent companion in those last weeks. As you were also very close to him I would appreciate your comment on the first stanza of a poem that I have written in honour of his memory.*

> I weep for Adonais – he is dead!
>   Oh weep for Adonais, though our tears
> Thaw not the frost which binds so dear a head!
>   And thou, sad Hour selected from all years
>   To mourn our loss, rouse thy obscure compeers,
> And teach them thine own sorrow! Say: "With me
>   Died Adonais! Till the future dares
> Forget the past, his fate and fame shall be
> An echo and a light unto eternity.[2]

STUDENTS' PAGE

What emotions and thoughts are revealed about the "Adonais" for whom the poem is written?

Finally, some details to help resolve the questions you need answered. What do you know about the chest and its contents now? You determine to keep a list of:
- facts,
- theories,
- suppositions based on evidence,
- 'just plain guesses' (needing more evidence), and
- additional questions that need answers.

You are able to unravel the pieces of yet another page on which a segment of poetry is found – this time more clearly written but in the style of the handwriting of the author of the "last will and testament".

> This living hand, now warm and capable
> Of earnest grasping, would, if it were cold
> And in icy silence of the tomb,
> So haunt thy days and chill thy dreaming nights
> That thou would wish thine own heart dry of blood
> So my veins red life might stream again,
> And thou be conscious-calmed – see here it is –
> I hold it towards you.[3]

Eight lines. The occasional word crossed out and corrections made suggest that this is a first and incomplete draft. No title, no name. What was the poet trying to say? Could this be a part of a much longer poem? What emotions are being felt by the author for him to have written such fearful lines?

You need to find some more names. When were these poems and letters written? Some firm evidence is needed. Could these writers have been contemporaries of John Donne or Shakespeare or did they write in a much later period of time? What qualities in the writing reveal an historical record of the authors? You should make some more notes under the listed headings. A little research now may save much time later.

You have not found a poem or letter that has been clearly signed identifying the author or the recipient. These men (are they all men?) were obviously known to each other and yet they remain a confusion to you. You slowly piece together another text using patience, curiosity and determination.

> Betwixt damnation and impassion'd clay
> Must I burn through; once more humbly assay
> The bitter-sweet of this Shakespearian fruit.
> Chief Poet! and ye clouds of Albion,
> Begetters of our deep eternal theme,
> When through the old oak forest I am gone,
> Let me not wander in a barren dream,
> But when I am consumed in the fire,
> Give me new Phoenix wings to fly at my desire.[4]

My Best Poetry Unit

STUDENTS' PAGE

There were five lines above these but they were unable to be read; a combination of tears in the folds of the paper and faded and smudged ink work. Is this a part of a sonnet? How is the mood of the poet revealed? What is suggested in these lines that can provide further evidence of authorship? It has the same handwriting as the last segment of poetry that you have already examined. Are there common qualities in the writing?

Once again you find a part of a letter wrapped within a sheaf of other papers. Many of these have faded past reading.

> *As to the poetical Character itself... it is not itself – it has no self – it is everything and nothing – It has no character – it enjoys light and shade; it lives in gusto, be it foul or fair, high or low, rich or poor, mean or elevated – It has as much delight in conceiving as Iago as an Imogen. What shocks the virtuous philosopher, delights the camelion Poet ...A Poet is the most unpoetical of anything in existence; because he has no Identity – he is continually in for – and filling some other Body – The Sun, The Moon, The Sea and Men and Women who are creatures of impulse are poetical and have about them as unchangeable attribute – the poet has none; no identity.*[5]

There are a number of qualities of the handwriting that clearly link these thoughts to the first author. However, the script displays greater confidence, conveying a youthful impression. This person is more sure of his views. What is he trying to say about the work of poets, or his own work?

You find another poem and this time the paper is folded on one of the edges of the text while the print has faded or simply disappeared in other segments of the text. Occasional words have been lost or blurred within the poem.[6]

```
_____ star! _____ I were as steadfa_____
 No ___ in lone splendour hung a _____ the _____
 And wa____ing, with eternal _____ apart,
 Li___ nature's ___tient, sleepless Eremite
 The moving waters at their priestlike task
 Of pure ablu____ round earth's human shores.
 Or gazing on the new soft-fallen m___k
  Of snow upon the _____ and the moors –
 No – yet still steadfast, still unchangeable,
  Pillowed on __.  _____ love's ripening breast,
 To feel forever its soft ____ll and swe___
  Awake for ever in a sweet unrest,
 _____, still to hear her tender tender-taken breath,
 ____ __ _____ ever – or else swoon to death.
```

Your first task is to attempt to fill the gaps. What words are missing? You determine to resolve these questions before going further. You feel that it is important to be able to note the reasons for the decisions that you make.

You discover another letter. This one is a complete page with occasional passages faded or illegible. There were obviously other pages but they are either yet to be uncovered or lost.

STUDENTS' PAGE

I have never yet been able to perceive how any thing can be known for truth by consequitive reasoning – and yet it must be– Can it be that even the greatest Philosopher ever arrived at his goals without putting aside numerous objections – However it may be, O for a Life of Sensations rather than of Thoughts! ... we shall enjoy ourselves here after by having what we call happiness on Earth repeated in a finer tone ... And yet such a fate can only befall those who delight in sensation rather than hunger as you do after Truth ...[7]

The author of this letter has expressed some critical views about his poetry. How do these thoughts compare with his earlier statements?

One of the final letters that you are able to piece together has a date, name and an author. Perhaps this letter will provide you with the necessary information to fill the gaps of information and knowledge about the contents of the chest.

21 October, 1819

My dearest Leigh

I have just been told of John's worsening health. As you are one of his most fervent supporters and I know that you take the greatest pleasure in providing benefaction t ...

(You cannot decipher the additional sentences in this paragraph.)

I am at once pleased and comforted that he heeded Percy's advice to leave our cold climes for the warmth of Italy.

(A number of unreadable paragraphs followed these opening sentences.)

I have heard that in the next edition of the Examiner you will publish a review of my most recent work on the English Comic Writers. I felt that these lectures were excessively pleasing and they may provide a wonderful distraction from the sadness of the news of John's worsening health.
I will write soon to relate to you my progress on a project I have planned with Byron.

Your most affectionate friend

William H

You are certain that this letter is a most important piece of the puzzle. You return to your list of facts, theories, suppositions based on the evidence and 'just plain guesses'. This final letter has allowed you to determine with more confidence many more details about the writing you have discovered. You wonder, was Leigh the owner of the chest? Who was he? Why would he have kept these letters and poems?

Conclusions

Consider all the information you have gathered.
1. What have you learnt about the poetry and the poets?
2. What have you learnt about the authors of the letters?

Discuss your answers to these questions with others.
3. Who has discovered the most information about the material presented?
4. How were their answers developed?
5. What sources did they use?
6. What additional information is required for you to answer all the questions you have considered?

TEACHER'S PAGE

Sequencing Activity (Years 9-12) — Richard Knott

Many of the activities that Lunzer and Gardner (*The Effective Use of Reading*, London: Heinemann 1979) brought together under the acronym DARTS (Directed Activities Related to Texts) have proved their worth when applied to poetry. Most teachers will have used a modified form of cloze, in which about half a dozen words are deleted from a poem and the students, in groups of two, three or four, decide on the most appropriate words to fill in the blanks. Each group's choices are then blackboarded, and the whole class votes on which suggestions seem the most appropriate. Then, and only then, is the original text revealed and subjected to critical scrutiny. Sometimes the class will decide that some of their choices are better than the poet's.

The sequencing activity using the poem *Green Beret* has provoked excellent discussion from Years 9 up to adult level. The final ten lines are in random order, and the pairs or threes (four is a little unwieldy for this activity) arrange the lines in which they regard as the best order. The activity is quite absorbing, requiring reading and re-reading the poem and discovering how the poet builds upon what has gone before. Different arrangements are possible, and the follow-up discussion will centre on which of the alternatives seems the best. The poet's own choice is then revealed:

> And the boy knew everything,
> He knew everything about them, the caves,
> the trails, the hidden places and the names,
> and in the moment that he cried out
> in that same instant,
> protected by frail tears
> far stronger than any wall of steel,
> they passed everywhere
> like tigers
> across the High Plateau.

The activity will be made easier if the students cut up their sheets so that each line is on a separate piece of paper.

(Adapted by permission of Richard Knott from his book, *The English Department in a Changing World* Milton Keynes: Open University Press, 1985.)

Sequencing Activity

In your group, read the first two stanzas of this poem two or three times. Then arrange the final ten lines in the order that your group feels is the best.

Green Beret

Ho Thien

Ho Thien of the 4th Plains Unit wrote this down sixty days after New Year, after hearing the story from a woman of Dalat on the High Plateau.

He was twelve years old,
and I do not know his name
The mercenaries took him and his father,
whose name I do not know,
one morning upon the High Plateau.
Green Beret looked down on the frail boy
with the eyes of a hurt animal and thought,
a good fright will make him talk.
He commanded, and the father was taken away
behind the forest's green wall.
'Right kid tell us where they are,
tell us where or your father – dead.'
With eyes now bright and filled with terror
the slight boy said nothing.
'You've got one minute left kid,' said Green Beret,
'tell us where or we kill father,'
and thrust his wrist watch against a face all eyes,
the second hand turning, jerking on its way.
'OK boy ten seconds to tell us where they are.'
In the last instant the silver hand shattered the sky
and the forest of trees.

'Kill the old guy,' roared Green Beret
and shots hammered out
behind the forest's green wall
and sky and trees and soldiers stood
in silence, and the boy cried out.
Green Beret stood
in silence, as the boy crouched down
and shook with tears,
as children do when their father dies.
'Christ,' said one mercenary to Green Beret
'he didn't know a damn thing
we killed the old guy for nothing.'
So they all went away,
Green Beret and his mercenaries.

STUDENTS' PAGE

Here are the final ten lines in random order:

like tigers

protected by frail tears

across the High Plateau.

and in the moment that he cried out

And the boy knew everything,

far stronger than any wall of steel,

the trails, the hidden places and the names,

they passed everywhere

He knew everything about them, the caves,

in that same instant,

TEACHER'S PAGE

Two Translations of a Tang Poem
(A workshop Approach) (Years 7-10) — Glenys Acland

Two modern English translations of a 1200-year-old Chinese poem from the Tang dynasty invite students of Years 7 to 10 to explore the translators' interpretations through group performances, through close examination of the poetic and musical qualities, and through contrasting the styles of the translators. One activity which helps students to examine the themes of the poem is exploring feelings surrounding farewells. This Li Bai (701-762) poem was titled *Saying Goodbye to My Friend*, by Tu An and Tu Di and *Farewell to a Friend* by Xu Yuanzhong.

Introductory Activities

Introduce the theme of the poem by having students brainstorm in groups of three or four and share with the class the possible feelings friends have when one of them leaves. Are there differences in the way the person who leaves feels from the way that the person who is left behind might feel?

The tone for working with a Chinese poem could be established by such means as playing Chinese music as students enter the class, displaying Chinese art, particularly works depicting panoramic landscapes, or viewing a portion of a Chinese opera, noting the elements: art, music, dance, acrobatics, masks and costumes.

With older students, the question could be posed: What are some of the rituals surrounding farewells in your culture – and in other cultures?

Dramatic Interpretations in a Performance

The two translations lend themselves to dramatic interpretation because of their sensuous language, contrasting treatments, lyrical qualities, simple theme, and natural images.

Divide the class into two major groups, each to study one translation, and subdivide each group into subgroups of up to five students. Groups working on each translation should work independently, both to ensure diversity of interpretation and to set the stage for surprise when students learn that they have been working on two translations of the same poem. After discussing the poem in their subgroups, one "Saying Goodbye" subgroup is assigned to create a short scene depicting what might have gone on **before** the action in the poem. One of the "Farewell" subgroups creates a scene depicting what might have happened **after** the action in the poem. The second set of subgroups for each translation prepare to perform a choral speaking rendition of each poem. In both cases, acting, dance, music, and sound effects should be used to develop the scene. (It is best if students are encouraged to memorise these short poems rather than read from the scripts.) A third subgroup might be assigned to create a large art mural depicting the details of the panoramic landscape described in the poem. These murals might be used as backdrops for the performances of the other subgroups.

Analyses following the presentations will be facilitated by videotaping the performances.

Post Performance Analyses

Questions such as the following might help students to learn from the performances.
1. What are your feelings about your performance and those of your group?
2. What did memorising, collaborating, and performing the poem and developing an imaginary scene add to your understanding of the poem?
3. Did watching the performance of the other translation of the poem help you to arrive at a fuller and richer understanding of the poem?

Exploring the Translations

The original poem was written about 750 AD, during the Tang Dynasty. Once each student has a copy of both poems, the following questions could be explored in small groups.
- Which elements (words, phrases, images, word order, subject matter) in these recent English translations suggest that these poems are translations rather than original poems?
- Which translation do you prefer and why?
- Using these two translations as a basis, speculate on the difficulties of translating poetry from one language to another and from one century to another.
- What indications are there that we should be sceptical about the accuracy of either translation? What implications does this have for our reading of other translated material?
- Choose words and phrases from each translation to illustrate what you perceive to be the feelings of the friend who leaves and the friend who is left behind.
- Would the translations have been more effective if there had been no attempt to use rhyme?
- Which translation do you consider to be the better? Why?

References

Tu An and Tu Di. *Saying Goodbye to My Friend*, (Translation). In 300 Tang Poems (1680. 1747, 1996). Volume XVI of the Chinese-English Bilingual Series of Chinese Classics. Shanghai: Wu Juntao.

Xu Yuanzhong (2000) *Farewell to a Friend*, (Translation). In A Bilingual Edition of 300 Tang Poems. (Translated and edited by Xu Yuanzhong, Beijing: Higher Education Press.)

Suggested material that could be used to help set the tone for studying the translations:

1. Books: *Art & Culture* (2001) Robert L Thorp,
   Richard Ellis Vinograd ISBN 0 8109 41451
   ISBN 0 13 088969 5: Harry Abrams Inc NY.

2. Video: *Farewell My Concubine* (1993) China/Hong Kong
   Readily available on the foreign film shelves (use the Chinese Opera scenes from this video).

3. Search the Internet.

Saying Goodbye to My Friend

The green mount before the northern city stands,
The clear river goes around the eastern lands.
We have to part now at this memorial place,
And you alone will have a remote domain to face.
Like a cloud, you wanderer may float here and there;
My deep affection for you the sunset should always bear.
We wave to each other and say goodbye.
The horse sadly gives out neigh and neigh.

Farewell to a Friend

Blue mountains bar the northern sky;
White river girds the eastern town,
Here is the place to say goodbye;
You'll drift like lonely thistledown.
With floating cloud you'll float away;
Like parting day, I'll part from you.
You wave your hand and go your way;
Your steed still neighs, "Adieu, adieu!"

TEACHER'S PAGE

Gallery Walk (Years 9-11) – Philip Allingham

NB The Gallery Walk procedure can, of course, be used with other poems. After the poem has been introduced (see below) and read aloud a couple of times, each pair of students is assigned a group of lines to work on, following the procedure outlined on the students' page. The questions produced in No 5 could be used in a follow-up activity known as a **person search**, in which students must elicit answers from others and obtain their signatures to indicate that, in each case, this was the answer given.

Class Choral Reading

Each pair of students can be asked to prepare their lines for a choral reading. They should be told to practise until they have made the choral reading a polished production. Tell them that they do not have to read all words in unison; they can experiment with reading some words together, pausing, and saying some words individually for emphasis. When all pairs are ready, a choral reading of the entire poem is performed.

Introducing the Poem

Harry Thurston's *Black Hull* (from a longer poem entitled *Atlantic Elegy*) is about the demise of the cod fishery and the social disruption to a way of life that goes back to the seventeenth century in Atlantic Canada. There are several ways of setting the context. The students might discuss the demise of a natural resource industry in their own area (eg, coal-mining) or the near-extinction of a species (eg, the buffalo on the American and Canadian Prairie) and its social consequences through a webbing exercise, or through a series of before-and-after pictures drawn from magazines and made into posters by small groups, with a series of adjectives under each picture (eg, "Before"–pristine, prosperous, colourful, optimistic; "After"–polluted, abandoned, lifeless, pessimistic). Or the teacher could read to the class the short story *The Boat* from Alistair Macleod's recent collection ***Island: The Collected Stories of Alistair Macleod*** (Toronto: McClelland & Stewart, 2001/ London: Jonathan Cape 2001).

Annotations

"Black Hull" may suggest a derelict, but is probably a reference to the tarring of a wooden boat to prevent damage by marine creatures such as barnacles. Black hulls with gold lettering were a distinctive feature of the Lunenberg, Nova Scotia, fleet of Grandbankers. Thurston, who lives in Tidnishbridge, Nova Scotia, is thinking of the Atlantic fishing industry in general, rather than simply that of Cape Breton or Newfoundland. This is definitely a 'have-not' area of Canada, heavily dependent on government relief programs.

"A widow's walk" is a small balcony with a railing on top of a house; one sees such structures in nineteenth-century houses in Atlantic Canada, and occasionally in coastal British Columbia. The structure gets its name from the notion that the wife might see her husband's ship limping into port and know that, this time, she has escaped being a widow – but there is always the possibility that the fishing vessel will never return, and she will pace the narrow walk for the rest of her days.

"Baccalieu" is a French and Portuguese way of salting Atlantic cod in order to preserve it for the homeward journey; in St. John's, Newfoundland, the drying racks for this process once covered a whole hillside – and raised a great stench! In this form, fishermen traded cod to the West Indies in return for sugar-cane (which became the potent "screech" rum back in Newfoundland) and other Caribbean products.

"Capelin" – an Atlantic fish that was extremely plentiful until the 1960s. It grows to a length of 40 cms, and spawns close inshore in swarming schools just below the surface. It is the principal diet of the much larger Atlantic cod; hence, if the numbers of capelin decline, so too do the cod.

Page 40   My Best Poetry Unit

Gallery Walk

Black Hull: from the long poem *Atlantic Elegy*

Harry Thurston

The sea is memory. Forests of masts
Growing in the harbours, white pine with sails
for leaves reefed, expectant as held breath.

Every mud creek bed cradled a keel,
every ocean hailed a bluenose captain,
every parlour blossomed with the exotic,
every rooftop sprouted a widow's walk;
sail lofts, foundries, insurance houses
stitched, hammered and brokered maritime dreams.

Then, black clouds smudged the white horizon,
in the end, fortunes rode the rails west.

Black hulls with their proud nameplates embossed
in gold raced from the Banks, close-reached for home.
Salt boxes filled with *baccalieu*, bartered
for rum. Men met their fate in yellow dories.

A gull's wing curved in the atomised air,
cracked hands carved a half model to cut waves,
Cape Islanders took shape from root and bole,
men christened them for wives and girl children.

Trawls outset hook-and-line, bulged with fish
thrown overboard, time after time. All
so some restauranteur could serve a fillet
the size of his palm caught to order,
some stockbroker could clip a coupon,
some politician could be elected.

Names old as the continent disappear,
Fishers, fish-cutters become eco-refugees.
Now we have remembrance, rust, and rot,
Bureaucracies and empty seas are our lot.

No longer do sage cod, big as gaffers
(Atlantic gods sporting pharaonic whiskers)
gather in our coves, waters thicken with eggs
like tapioca, beaches bear witness to the strange love-making of capelin.

Seabirds drown in bilge oil, brass propellers
split open the last whales, fish spawn tumours.
We scrape the bottom for urchin, pick winkles,
dig bloodworms, strip the very rocks for weed,
in despair burn boats to the waterline–
wait, wait for what may never come again.

Gallery Walk

Instructions

1. Choose a colour of poster paper appropriate to the **mood** of your passage.

2. Re-copy your lines in large print on the poster paper, using a different colour or style of print for important words. You may use another colour to make marginal observations.

3. Select a key image from your passage and illustrate it on your poster paper.

4. Choose an appropriate title for your poster from the passage: a startling phrase, image, or an important word (you need not use words from the poem).

5. Put your names at the very bottom of the poster, and include what you feel is an interpretative question which can be answered from reading the poem. Write the answer on the reverse side of your poster paper.

6. Display your poster in the spot designated by the teacher so that it is positioned in the correct spot in the sequence of lines.

7. Be prepared to read out and explain your assigned lines and poster. You will have to field questions from the rest of the class and ask your question at the bottom of the poster.

8. Rate the quality of your work on the following scale:
   Poor – Average – Good
   A. neatness and accuracy of transcription of lines: 1 2 3 4 5
   B. degree of co-operation between presenters: 1 2 3 4 5
   C. overall effectiveness of presentation: 1 2 3 4 5
   D. ability to explain poster and answer questions: 1 2 3 4 5
   TOTAL =   /20

TEACHER'S PAGE

Extended Metaphors 1 – (Years 9-10) – Wendy Jonas

The Human Exhibition

In these unit students will:

❖ encounter language used by modern poets and by Shakespeare four hundred years' ago;

❖ focus on imagery, especially the technique of the **extended metaphor**;

❖ use the poems as a stimulus for their own writing or composing.

1. A number of pictures (people of varying ages, races, appearance, facial expressions; from past and modern times) are circulated for students working in small groups to respond to and discuss. Examples:

    ❖ Portraits by artists: **Van Eyck's** *Arnolfini Wedding Portrait*, **Bruegel's** *The Old Shepherd*, **da Vinci's** *Young Woman with an Ermine*, **Vermeer's** *The Lacemaker*, **Cézanne's** *Man With a Pipe*, **Dobell's** *Billy Boy, Joshua Smith, Dame Mary Gilmore*.

    ❖ Photographs: old and modern, for example, babies, brides, family groups, school photos.

    ❖ Pictures from newspapers and magazines or CD covers: emphasis on the ordinary as well as the unusual or interesting.

2. Thiele's poem *Portraits* is then issued and read. In their groups, students prepare for whole class discussion a list of questions about any aspect of the poem not understood.

3. The term **metaphor** and the concept of **extended metaphor** are explained and discussed. Working in their small groups, students then:

    ❖ find all the details in the poem (words, phrases or lines; ideas and images) connected with the idea of an art gallery and the paintings or drawings of people which it exhibits;

    ❖ discuss why they think the poet used this extended metaphor; what they think he is saying;

    ❖ write **no more than two or three sentences** in which **without using the metaphor** they try to express, in their own words, what the poet is saying about the people all around us – the poem's main idea.

4. **Writing Task:** Each student selects from his/her own experience
    a) a person who is one of the "familiar faces" seen "each day".
    b) a person not well-known, perhaps seen or met only once, ie, a "glimpsed sketch", and writes a brief 'portrait' of each. These descriptions should not concentrate on appearance only but might try to capture some "aspect, mood, belief" which makes or made the subject interesting.

My Best Poetry Unit

Extended Metaphors

Portraits

Colin Thiele

Humanity remains its own strange gallery –
Each day hung with familiar faces
And those glimpsed sketches
As vaguely disturbing as half-remembered places.

Some, full face, we know but never see,
And some – so great the art –
Haunt our life's history,
Or, like old canvases, cracked and curled,
From a sudden niche astound the inmost heart.
People, fleshed in fact or fantasy,
Ring round the gaze we give the world.

The light and shadow of their native selves
Shaded and lit by aspect, mood, belief,
Catch moments of truth – like chance
Sketches in charcoal and conté –
That fill the frames of circumstance.

Comic or tragic, each in turn reveals
The variousness of man's condition.
The doors are always open on the human exhibition.

Extended Metaphors 2 – (Years 9-10) – Wendy Jonas

Life as a Stage

1. The concept of **extended metaphor** is revised. Shakespeare's metaphor in *All the World's a Stage* is introduced by focusing on the first four lines and the whole is then read . . .

2. Working in small groups, students prepare a list of questions they want answered and these are dealt with in whole class discussion.

3. In their groups students list the "seven ages" or 'parts played' in the lifetime of a man or woman of the twenty-first century. (After this activity Bruce Dawe's *Enter Without So Much as Knocking*, which traces the life of a modern man from birth to death, could be read and compared.[1])

4. **Writing Task:** Each student chooses one of the "ages" of Shakespeare (or Dawe) – Childhood, Old Age, The Lover etc – as the title for a piece of writing using any approach, for example, narrative, reflective, descriptive and any tone, eg, serious or light-hearted and humorous.

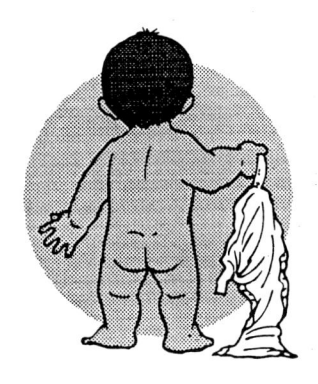

---

1. Bruce Dawe, *Sometimes Gladness: Collected Poems 1954-82* Melbourne: Longman Cheshire, revised edition, 1983.

All the World's a Stage

William Shakespeare

As You Like It II vii 139-166

All the world's a stage,
And all the men and women merely players.
They have their exits and their entrances;
And one man in his time plays many parts,
His acts being seven ages. At first the infant,
Mewling and pewking in the nurse's arms.
And then the whining school-boy, with his satchel
And shining morning face, creeping like snail
Unwillingly to school. And then the lover,
Sighing like furnace, with a woeful ballad
Made to his mistress' eyebrow. Then a soldier,
Full of strange oaths and bearded like the pard,
Jealous in honour, sudden and quick in quarrel,
Seeking the bubble reputation
Even in the cannon's mouth. And then the justice,
In fair round belly with good capon lined,
With eyes severe and beard of formal cut,
Full of wise saws and modern instances;
And so he plays his part. The sixth age shifts
Into the lean and slippered pantaloon,
With spectacles on nose and pouch on side,
His youthful hose, well saved, a world too wide
For his shrunk shank; and his big manly voice,
Turning again toward childish treble, pipes
And whistles in his sound. Last scene of all,
That ends this strange eventful history,
Is second childhood and mere oblivion,
Sans teeth, sans eyes, sans taste, sans everything.

TEACHER'S PAGE

Comparing Two Versions (Years 10-12) – Matthew Brown

1. Make a copy of the original version of *La Belle*. Cut copies of the poem into its various stanzas. Have the class work in small groups. Each group should try to arrange the stanzas in a logical and 'poetic' order. They should be able to justify the order that they establish.
   a) Compare the different arrangements of the stanzas that each group creates.
   b) Have each group read their version aloud.
   c) Which version was preferred? Why? (Refer to these versions of the poem for later questions.)

2. Distribute the original version of the *La Belle*. Have the original poem read aloud. What did you like about it? What were your impressions?
   a) In what different ways can the poem be read aloud? Have different students adopt different tones in reading the opening stanzas.
   b) Consider reading this poem aloud to different audiences. What changes in tone might be adopted?

3. The translation of the poem's title is "Beautiful woman without mercy" or "The Lovely Lady without Pity" – Why do you believe the poet has chosen to use French for the title?

4. Work in small groups. Have them read the poem again. Ask them:
   a) What do you see? What do you hear? What do you feel?
   b) What examples of language helped you make some meaning in the poem?
   c) Where is the poet taking you? (Where has the poet taken you?)
   d) What do you think the original poem is about? Have each person in the group give his/her impressions of the poem.
   e) In your groups write a list of questions about the poem that you would like answered.
   f) Read these questions to the class. Note common questions and ask why these questions emerge as common concerns. Members of the class may attempt to answer questions from the groups as they are listed on the board.

5. Have the students consider their response to the following questions:
   a) Who is speaking to whom? Is it always the same person speaking? What moments in the poem lead you to this conclusion?
   b) What is the knight searching for? Will he be successful in his search? How do you know?
   c) Is the woman/lady "without mercy"?

6. The poem is written as a ballad. What are the qualities of a ballad? Is this an effective form of poetry? Be prepared to justify your response.

TEACHER'S PAGE

7. Introduce the class to the revised edition. Have each student highlight the differences between the two poems on the revised copy of *La Belle Dame Sans Merci*.
   a) What are the most significant changes between the poems?
      i) changes in words
      ii) grammar
      iii) order of stanzas
   b) How much difference do the changes in grammar make between the two poems? Comment on the examples listed below:

Original Poem	**Revised Poem**
Alone and palely loitering?	Alone and palely loitering;
And no birds sing!	And no birds sing.
And there I dream'd – Ah woe betide!	And there I dream'd, ah woe betide,
I saw pale Kings, and Princes too	I saw pale kings, and princes too,
On the cold hill's side.	On the cold hill side.
And no birds sing–	And no birds sing.

   c) Read the second poem aloud. Do the changes become more apparent in the reading of the poems?
   d) Have the students choose their preferred version for each change made by Keats. Each preference needs to be justified. Has making these choices created a third poem?
   e) How significant is the altering of the order of the stanzas in the middle of the poem? Is the meaning altered? Consider the versions of the original poem that various groups had devised for the first question.
   f) Critics almost universally prefer the original edition of the poem. Which version is the better?

8. The original *La Belle* was written in April, 1819 and published in the *Indicator* in 1820. The revised poem was sent to George and Georgiana Keats as part of letter. When the editors of the *Indicator* published the revised edition in 1848 one critic believes it was a response to the notion that the original *La Belle* was "too sentimental".
   a) What is meant here by 'sentimental'?
   b) What elements of the original poem might suggest that it was more 'sentimental'?
   c) Is sentimentality a flaw?

Comparing Two Versions

La Belle Dame Sans Merci (Original)
John Keats

O what can ail thee, Knight-at-arms,
   Alone and palely loitering?
The sedge is wither'd from the Lake,
   And no birds sing!

O what can ail thee, Knight-at-arms,
   So haggard and so woe-begone?
The Squirrel's granary is full,
   And the harvest's done.

I see a lily on thy brow,
   With anguish moist and fever dew;
And on thy cheek a fading rose
   Fast withereth too–

I met a Lady in the meads
   Full beautiful, a faery's child
Her hair was long, her foot was light,
   And her eyes were wild–

I made a Garland for her head,
   And bracelets too, and fragrant Zone;
She look'd at me as she did love,
   And made sweet moan–

I set her on my pacing steed,
   And nothing else saw all day long;
For sidelong would she bend and sing
   A faery's song–

She found me roots of relish sweet,
   And honey wild, and manna dew;
And sure in language strange she said,
   I love thee true–

She took me to her elfin grot,
   And there she wept, and sigh'd full sore,
And there I shut her wild wild eyes–
   With kisses four.

And there she lulled me asleep
   And there I dream'd – Ah woe betide!
The latest dream I ever dreamt
   On the cold hill side.

I saw pale Kings, and Princes too
   Pale warriors, death-pale were they all;
They cried, La belle dame sans merci
   Hath thee in thrall!

I saw their starv'd lips in the gloam
   With horrid warning gaped wide,
And I awoke, and found me here
   On the cold hill's side.

And this is why I sojourn here
   Alone and palely loitering;
Though the sedge is withered from the Lake,
   And no birds sing–

La Belle Dame Sans Merci (Revised)
John Keats

Ah, what can ail thee, wretched wight,
   Alone and palely loitering;
The sedge has wither'd from the Lake,
   And no birds sing.

Ah, what can ail thee, wretched wight,
   So haggard and so woe-begone?
The squirrel's granary is full,
   And the harvest's done.

I see a lily on thy brow,
   With anguish moist and fever dew;
And on thy cheek a fading rose
   Fast withereth too.

I met a Lady in the meads
   Full beautiful, a fairy's child;
Her hair was long, her foot was light,
   And her eyes were wild.

I set her on my pacing steed,
   And nothing else saw all day long;
For sideways would she lean, and sing
   A faery's song.

I made a garland for her head,
   And bracelets too, and fragrant zone;
She look'd at me as she did love,
   And made sweet moan.

She found me roots of relish sweet,
   And honey wild, and manna dew;
And sure in language strange she said,
   I love thee true.

She took me to her elfin grot,
   And there she gaz'd and sighed deep,
And there I shut her wild sad eyes–
   So kiss'd to sleep.

And there we slumber'd on the moss,
   And there I dream'd, ah woe betide,
The latest dream I ever dream'd
   On the cold hill side.

I saw pale kings, and princes too,
   Pale warriors, death-pale were they all;
Who cry'd – "La belle Dame sans merci
   Hath thee in thrall!"

I saw their starv'd lips in the gloam
   With horrid warning gaped wide,
And I awoke, and found me here
   On the cold hill side.

And this is why I sojourn here
   Alone and palely loitering,
Though the sedge is wither'd from the lake,
   And no birds sing.

My Best Poetry Unit

Poem and Paintings

Consider the two artworks titled *La Belle Dame sans Merci*, the first by the artist, Sir Frank Dicksee (1853-1928) the second by John William Waterhouse (1849-1917). The Dicksee painting may be found on the web at

> http://www.artmagick.com/ALLpaintings/dicksee/dicksee1.jpg

and the Waterhouse at

> http://www.artmagick.com/paintings/painting1452.asp

There are a number of artists who have been drawn to Keats's poem as a source for inspiration. Sometimes, once viewed, an artist's portrayal supports our view of the original work and occasionally we are so drawn by the artist's work that we are overwhelmed by the poem's transformation.

a) What atmosphere is captured in Dicksee's painting?

b) How does the atmosphere of Waterhouse's painting differ from that created by Dicksee?

c) Find lines from each poem which are most clearly reflected in these art works. Are some lines better represented in one painting than another? Be prepared to give reasons for your choices.

d) Is one version of the poem more accurately portrayed in these paintings?

e) Does viewing these paintings enhance your understanding or appreciation of the poem?

f) Having examined these artworks, is your view of *La Belle Dame sans Merci* forever shaped by these artist's realisations of the poem?

g) Keats is a "Romantic" poet. What does this term mean?
What elements of these artworks support this view?

h) Have the artists mirrored your own view of the poem and the poet's intent?
Which of the artworks more effectively represents the poet's intent?

TEACHER'S PAGE

Mapping Responses to a Poem (Years 9-12)
Michael & Peter Benton

In recent decades, exploratory, informal writing as an aid to reading and understanding has developed widespread applications in English teaching. Nowhere is it more helpful than in poetry teaching. Poems are cast in the most precise and concrete forms of language that we have, yet reading them they can often seem, at first, to be just a blur of words. Their language needs time for the images, ideas and feelings to be assimilated. Re-readings, copying out the texts, monitoring one's own thoughts in brief jottings – all slow down the reading process and provide the mental space for reflection that poems demand. The approach suggested below through the example *Cock-Crow* aims first to engage the individual reader with the text, not with a pressure towards value judgements, but as a means of representing to oneself the ideas and feelings that accompany initial readings. Subsequently, such notes may lead to group/class discussion and to more considered written work. Throughout, the essential message remains: a student's individual responses to poems are both valid and valued.

Editor's note:

Michael and Peter Benton are the authors of several important anthologies and of other books on the teaching of poetry, particularly **Examining Poetry** (London: Hodder & Stoughton, 1986), which contains a chapter, 'Making Your Own Notes Around a Poem'. Teachers are particularly recommended to their three anthologies linking poetry and painting, all published by Hodder & Stoughton:

- *Double Vision* (1990)
- *Painting With Words* (1995)
- *Picture Poems* (1997)

Their other anthologies include:

- *New Touchstones First* (2000)
- *New Touchstones 11-14* (1998)
- *New Touchstones 14-16* (1998)
- *New Touchstones Advanced* (In preparation, due 2002)

Michael Benton is the author of *Studies in the Spectator Role. Literature, Painting & Pedagogy*, (London: Routledge 2000).

STUDENTS' PAGE

Mapping Responses to a Poem

Every reading of a poem is a different 'performance', whether we read it ourselves or hear someone else do so. It is rather like hearing music we already know. We often find something new or different each time we listen. So it is with poems. The same words are in the same order on the page – they don't change any more than the notes in a musical score – but our performances change. Not only will there be different 'readings' from one person to the next, but there will be variations when we read a poem for a second or third time.

One way to discover how you read poems and to see how your thoughts differ from, or overlap with, those of other readers is to plot your thought-track in note form around the text. With short poems, as in *Cock-Crow* below, it is best to write out the poem on a single sheet of paper. The act of copying the text begins the process of getting inside the poem, with one thought leading to the next as in this annotated example. Try it for yourself with a poem of your choice.

1st thought
- being woken up by two cocks crowing together
- last line — let down feeling / just getting light

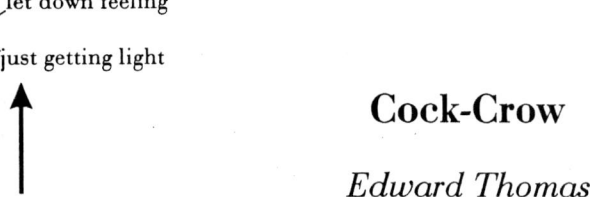

2nd thoughts on re-reading
- why 'wood of thoughts'?
- I like the *sounds* – words and rhymes.
- image chain: wood grows/ cut down/axe/cleave/silver blow
- visual impact of heraldic tableau.

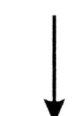

6th thoughts
- carefully worked regular shape: 2 long lines, alt. with broken line. Useful esp. in 'Heralds ... hand, Each ... each' = framed.

Cock-Crow
Edward Thomas

Out of the wood of thoughts that grows by night
To be cut down by the sharp axe of light,
Out of the night, two cocks together crow,
Cleaving the darkness with a silver blow:
And bright before my eyes twin trumpeters stand,
Heralds of splendour, one at either hand,
Each facing each as in a coat of arms:
The milkers lace their boots up at the farms.

3rd thoughts
relation of world in his head and world outside = between visual images and sound of cock-crow.

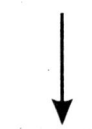

5th thoughts
lots of opposites like this:
the world ... the real world
inside his head ... *outside*
thoughts ... actions
night ... light
growth ... cutting down
darkness ... silver

4th thoughts re last 4 lines
contrast between
static ... moving
near, local ... distanced
stylised ... earthy, everyday
colourful ... colourless
noble ... peasant

Page 52   My Best Poetry Unit

TEACHER'S PAGE

Teaching *Kubla Khan* (Years 10-12) — Ernie Tucker

As this is perhaps the most celebrated, even notorious of poems, I like to teach this in Year 11 to give students the idea that ambiguity may be a very positive thing in poetry. Here, too, in the large bibliography is evidence of disputed readings, from T S Eliot's dismissal of the poem as of 'exaggerated repute' to Coleridge's own frustration at his inability to finish this 'fragment'.

Because of this wealth of material (Coleridge himself left more than 2000 letters and 80 notebooks) I use *Kubla Khan* to enable the students to exercise their preferences according to their learning styles and other interests. I prefer a group approach which gives real responsibility to each group as their tasks are quite different and the class will depend on their findings.

The notoriety of the poem allows me to start with a 'What do we already know about this poet, his times and his poem?' before moving on to 'What do we need to know?'. During the group investigations and at the end, in the evaluation lesson, my role as teacher is to point up any gaps that need filling and add an amusing cross-reference to A D Hope's poem *Persons from Porlock*.

Often I commence a series of lessons with my own reading aloud performance, except in the case of *The Rime of the Ancient Mariner* where I cannot compete with Richard Burton's cracks and growls, roars and howls. However, with *Kubla Khan* I prefer a dramatic reading to come at the end and be prepared by a group of students who have chosen this task. This approach avoids any dry-as-dust discussions lifted from the cribs and critics about the best rhythms and tones for the reading.

The next group are the researchers who set off for the library and the internet following the 'What we know/need to know session'. As we don't have six weeks to do this, some issues of relevance have to be decided upon. 'What we know' inevitably brings up the opium dream question. Was this an urban myth? Something used by Coleridge's enemies? Who was Kubla Khan and how did Coleridge get to know of him? What's a dulcimer? Why Abyssinian? How many domes are there? How did this poem become so famous? When did Coleridge write this? Where was Coleridge at this time? How old was he? Was he already famous? What else/who else influenced his writing?

We all have art students in our classes and their contribution to the language arts aspects of English is too often neglected. Their talents in drawing and preferred visual learning styles greatly assist English lessons. They often have a superior knowledge of history and culture through art history lessons and gallery visits. To harness these skills and experiences, I set up two groups to draw the poem, one to more or less map the river Alph and the other to choose sections to sketch to bring together in a wall display which will interpret the poem to the rest of the class.

The map task (unfortunately geography students are a rare breed) inevitably begins to produce an exotic map of the kind where dragons, whales and sea serpents dwelt in the margins. Yet Coleridge was writing in the great age of map-makers such as James Cook.

TEACHER'S PAGE

We usually get from the exotic to the Gothic via someone's drawing of the 'woman wailing for her demon-lover' and thus to questions of the various oppositions: holy/enchanted, sun/ice, dome/cave, and if our research group doesn't come up with others such as Alph(a)/omega, finite/infinite, Romantic/Rationalist, East/West, then that's where I come in. In any case, this is very enjoyable and leads to lots of out-of-class talk and comments from other classes who also use the same classroom. I'll always remember one girl's interpretation of the walls and towers with their 'gardens bright with sinuous rills / Where blossomed many an incense-bearing tree', reminding me not of the ordered gardens of Coleridge's 1797 but the thorns overcoming Sleeping Beauty's castle.

After each group has reported, I ask them to select the most important two lines and justify their choice. How do you build a dome with music, let alone one built 'in air'? If these discussions don't give me the problematic lines 'And 'mid this tumult Kubla heard from far / Ancestral voices prophesying war!' then the A D Hope poem will do the trick: 'Amid this tumult Kubla heard from far / Voices of Porlock babbling round the bar.'

It's a fun way to end the lessons after the research group has revealed all about Coleridge and his influences and the performance group has argued their case for their interpretation and we've all seen the merits of ambiguity.

'It was unfortunate: Poor S T C . . .
He knew the words by rote,
Had but to set them down . . .'

References

1. T S Eliot *The Use of Poetry and the Use of Criticism* (London, Faber and Faber, 1964 p146.
2. A D Hope *Persons from Porlock* in A D Hope *Selected Poems* (Sydney: Angus & Robertson, 1992, pp59-60.)
3. An accessible biography for students is:
   Cornwell, David *Coleridge Poet and Revolutionary 1772-1804* (London Allen Lane Penguin Books, 1973.)
4. See also:
   Holmes, Richard *Coleridge: Early Visions* (London: Harper Collins, 1989),
   Coleridge: Darker Reflections (London Harper Collins, 1998).
5. There is a pop-up version of the poem by the artist Nick Bantock (Viking Penguin, 1994).

Kubla Khan
Samuel Taylor Coleridge

In Xanadu did Kubla Khan
A stately pleasure-dome decree:
Where Alph, the sacred river, ran
Through caverns measureless to man
 Down to a sunless sea.
So twice five miles of fertile ground
With walls and towers were girdled round:
And there were gardens bright with sinuous rills,
Where blossomed many an incense-bearing tree;
And here were forests ancient as the hills,
Enfolding sunny spots of greenery.
But oh! that deep romantic chasm which slanted
Down the green hill athwart a cedarn cover!
A savage place! as holy and enchanted
As e'er beneath a waning moon was haunted
By woman wailing for her demon-lover!
And from this chasm, with ceaseless turmoil seething,
As if this earth in fast thick pants were breathing,
A mighty fountain momently was forced:
Amid whose swift half-intermitted burst
Huge fragments vaulted like rebounding hail,
Or chaffy grain beneath the thresher's flail:
And 'mid these dancing rocks at once and ever
It flung up momently the sacred river.
Five miles meandering with a mazy motion
Through wood and dale the sacred river ran,
Then reached the caverns measureless to man,
And sank in tumult to a lifeless ocean:
And 'mid this tumult Kubla heard from far
Ancestral voices prophesying war!

    The shadow of the dome of pleasure
    Floated midway on the waves;
    Where was heard the mingled measure
    From the fountain and the caves.
It was a miracle of rare device,
A sunny pleasure-dome with caves of ice!

A damsel with a dulcimer
In a vision once I saw:
It was an Abyssinian maid,
And on her dulcimer she played,
Singing of Mount Abora.
Could I revive within me
Her symphony and song,
To such a deep delight 'twould win me,
That with music loud and long,
I would build that dome in air,
That sunny dome! Those caves of ice!
And all who heard should see them there,
And all should cry, Beware! Beware!
His flashing eyes, his floating hair!
Weave a circle round him thrice,
And close your eyes with holy dread,
For he on honey-dew hath fed,
And drunk the milk of Paradise.

The Pictorial Essay (Years 9-11)
Trevor Gambell & Sam Robinson

The pictorial essay is, of course, appropriate for younger students as well, but these poems are best used with Years 9-11.

An alternative activity for *At the Wedding* is offered on page 60.

STUDENTS' PAGE

The Pictorial Essay

Create a pictorial essay as your response to one of these poems. A pictorial essay consists of images and words which can be cut out of printed materials (magazines, newspapers, catalogues – not books!) selected from photograph albums, copied from the internet, or images created by computer. You might include your own drawings, and you might select words from the poem to go with the images.

White Dresses

Rhona McAdam

It was supposed to be romantic. It was supposed to be
an easy thing, this flight into the big world
of men and women dancing on polished floors. Instead,
of course instead, it was a parade
through the staff lounge under the eye of the headmistress,
who checked skirt lengths for decency's sake;
instead of a respite from uniform
it was the substitution of white dresses
for green tunics. On the bus, seeking the dark-eyed
lustre of glamour, we became furtive cosmeticians,
glowing whitely through the night, dextrous
with mascara and rouge by flashlight.

At the boys' school we spilled from the bus,
incandescent in the light from the gym's open door,
lurching across gravel on feet more accustomed to oxfords.
We glowed against the wall bars with sweat and rouge,
mimicking steps in the shadows, awaiting discovery
and the fearful sheen of the dance floor.

Sooner or later we were led out to the bushes
where our dresses glowed indiscreetly
and we tasted gin and cigarettes
the better to glide into the rough hands of rugby players,
press lips and braces against lips and braces,
perhaps allow small indiscretions of touch,
exchange names and grades, home towns,
then tottered back into the gym where sooner or later
the last waltz, the last grope,
the bored chaperone's beckoning hand
as the last of us were cut from the milling, suited forms
who turned pink faces and hands

up to the school bus windows, waving from the shadows
as we jerked and tumbled into the night
to fib and gossip and begin the long hope for phone calls.

At the Wedding

Andrew Wreggitt

The old farmer sits on the stage of the community hall
His feet dangle like plumb lines,
thick black shoes
swaying slowly to the music
His boys are on the dance floor
Their blond heads stick out in the crowd
like shafts of wheat
Five of them, the last one married today,
all of them living in different cities

He remembers each of them, fighting him,
running off to become what they are,

salesmen, doctors, city-dwellers
Even now, the old suspicion still in their faces
Quick to argue
over chores or raising children
He watches them moving in their white shirts,
their wives smiling and small children
tugging at their pant-legs

He knows now that he loves them
impossibly, for the arguments and the hard words
for being young and insolent
like a field of stones coaxed into grain
He wonders if they love him the same way,
with hindsight, with a farmer's suspicion of elements,
the unsureness they learned from him

He wishes now that one of them
would come and sit with him
up here on the stage,
touch his shoulder and talk
about the farm, or anything
He wishes now that he had loved them
always, as surely
as he loves them now

An Alternative Activity for *At the Wedding*

Andrew Wreggitt's sympathetic portrayal of an old farmer gives you an insight into the love, albeit in hindsight, the man feels for his five sons. What you don't know is how the sons feel about their father. Take on the identity of one of the sons. Not much is known about the sons, except that they are all married adults with children. They also live in cities. The poet mentions doctors and salesmen, but that does not necessarily account for all the sons' occupations.

This gives you an opportunity to create the life of one of the sons. The setting is the same: the wedding dance. Using either a journal entry or a free verse poem, explore one son's relationship with his father. In addition to the details that come from your imagination, your character portrait should be based on information gained from *At the Wedding*. For example, we know that the father and sons disagreed in the past and continue to argue over the chores and the right way to raise children. Exchange writings with another student. Use the Reader Response form below to react to your partner's writing.

Reader Response Form

Writer's Name:_____ Reader's Name _____

The word/phrase/line/sentence/passage I like best is _____

_____

because_____

_____

_____

I would like more information about_____

_____

because_____

_____

_____

Two words or phrases I would use to describe your portrait of the son are:

i._____ ii._____

Two words or phrases I would use to describe the son's feelings about his father are:

i._____ ii._____

The most original part of your writing is_____

_____

Teaching Post-Colonial Poems (Years 9-11)
Philip Allingham

Approaches to *History Lesson*

I would suggest three possible ways to introduce the poem. The first requires a good deal of the preparation by the teacher; the others are far simpler.

A. The teacher begins by opening up a discussion of the stereotypical view of North America's aboriginal peoples (and of other such groups) that the poem addresses. This can be done by showing video clips from some of the many films that deal with the early colonial period. Such widely available videos as *The Last of Mohicans, A Man Called Horse, Little Big Man, 1492, Dances with Wolves* and *Black Robe* all offer colonial perspectives on the North American Indian, and have significant moments worthy of analysis and response. Just a few minutes from each film with specific groups of students directed to analyse each sequence is a good warm-up to an informed reading of the poem. In particular, groups should address such questions as:
   1. According to the film, are aboriginal people clever or stupid? Explain.
   2. According to the film, what are the aboriginal people's motivations? Explain what the film shows them wanting.
   3. Does the film take a generally negative or positive view of the aboriginal way of life? Explain with reference to what you saw on the film.
   4. What is the role of women in traditional aboriginal society, according to the film?
   5. How does the film suggest that white people were justified in moving onto Indian land?

   After the teacher has led a reading of the poem *The History Lesson* from an overhead, each group should revisit its answers to the film questions, discussing how the poem offers an alternative perspective. Finally, each group should consider how each of the following elements is used in the poem to communicate its central idea: hyperbole, surrealism, repetition, pathos, irony, comic juxtaposition, present participles (I suggest each group be given a different device as its focus).

B. Begin with a basic blackboard overhead-projector exercise that gets the students to focus on the words "North American Indian" and "history" and elicits from them everything those words bring to mind; the idea, of course, is to get the students to connect the two bubbles by telling what they know. An interesting paired-poster project would be to have students work with magazine clippings and gluesticks to produce their own visual "history lessons". On the back of the poster the creators could write out what they feel the "lesson" of their poster is. The posters could then be displayed around the room, and the pairs of students could do a gallery walk, analysing everybody else's posters and providing simple statements of the "lessons" others' posters teach. This exercise would naturally lead in senior grades to a more formal consideration of the terms "theme" and "moral"- how the two are sometimes similar, but also how they differ.

C. Remove the poem's title and hand it out to groups of three. Working in groups, students will:
1. Read the poem aloud.
2. Jot down significant words that stand out after the reading.
3. Write down images or mental pictures that the poem has created.
4. Listen to the poem being read to the whole class.
5. Review words and images already jotted down, adding to these if necessary.
6. Devise a title for the poem, providing a justification .
7. Have one group member read out the proposed title and the justification.
8. Respond to the teacher's revealing the real title, possibly by:
    a. discussing as a group how that title has affected the group's interpretation of the poem, and generating a group paragraph; OR
    b. showing how the group's proposed title is superior to the actual title in a group-generated paragraph; OR
    c. showing how the real title is superior to the group's proposed title; OR
    d. individually writing a paragraph that compares the effectiveness of the two titles (to be submitted next class).

Follow Up

Students can list words and phrases that have religious associations, and then discuss in their groups the attitude to the Christian religion conveyed in the poem. What is the significance of this to the overall theme?

Notes:

Seagrams – a brand of whisky

'Flower-powered zee' – Zee Toilet tissue was advertised in North America as sweet-smelling and good for the environment. The advertisers hoped to link it with the 1960s 'flower-power' movement.

A musical setting of the poem by the group 'My Revolutionary' is available on Cargo Records CD and cassette.

Approaches to *Columbus*

The juxtaposition of European notions of wealth – exotic "gold pagodas" and slaves – and the true wealth of the earth, the beauty of flamingos and rivers, provides an interesting tension in this poem about the dubious rewards of Western acquisitiveness. The poem depends upon the reader's filling in the blanks to create meaning (for example, what is the connection between "conquistadors" and "spices" and "syphilis"?), making demands upon the reader's prior knowledge and ability to make connections. Even if the reader possesses the vocabulary necessary for a literal decoding of such lines as "When enough naked harbours had been manacled", the reader must ponder the metaphorical aspects of Hull's usage: for example, how can harbours be "naked" and "manacled"? The poem, therefore, lends itself to a pair-and-share brainstorming session in which each pair of students has to try to generate both literal and connotative readings of a different pair of lines, displaying what they have developed on poster paper. When these posters are assembled in the order of the lines they gloss, something of what Robert Hull is getting at will emerge.

Students will want to make a comparison between the two poems, particularly in relation to theme and tone.

Post-Colonial Poems

History Lesson

Jeannette Armstrong

Out of the belly of Chrisopher's ship
a mob bursts
Running in all directions
Pulling furs off animals
Shooting buffalo
Shooting each other
left and right

Father mean well
waves his makeshift wand
forgives saucer-eyed Indians

Red coated knights
gallop across the prairie
to get their men
and to build a new world

Pioneers and traders
bring gifts
Smallpox, Seagrams
and rice krispies

Civilisation has reached
the promised land

Between the snap crackle pop
of smoke stacks
and multicoloured rivers
swelling with flower powered zee
are farmers sowing skulls and bones
and miners
pulling from gaping holes
green paper faces
of a smiling English lady

The colossi
in which they trust
while burying
breathing forests and fields
beneath concrete and steel
stand shaking fists
waiting to mutilate
whole civilisations
ten generations at a blow

Somewhere among the remains
of skinless animals
is the termination
to a long journey
and unholy search
for the power
glimpsed in a garden
forever closed
forever lost

Columbus

Robert Hull

'Generally it was my wish to pass no island
without taking possession of it.'

The slaves were not profitable
'for almost half of them died'

but there were spears to be had
for broken crockery

and untouched rings of islets
like trinkets.

And though the Great Khan
finally went missing

and the gold pagodas
faded with the mists

there was the first flamingo
pink as dawn

there was the terminal innocence
of rivers.

When enough naked harbours
had been manacled

enough grief
requisitioned

a cargo of fables
set out for Spain, heavy

with lilting names –
Cathay Indies

conquistadors spices
syphilis

TEACHER'S PAGE

An Introduction to Literary Theory (Years 10-12)
Mark Howie

Introduction

The unit of work which follows was developed for a Year 10 class with a view to preparing the students for senior work. It introduced them to Literary Theory in what proved to be an accessible and engaging manner. In establishing the context for the unit with the class in the first lessons, the following quotation proved most useful:

> *(Literary) Theory ... involves a shift from a concern with what individual texts mean to a concern with textuality, that is, a concern with the ways in which texts are constructed and the ways in which readers negotiate with them to produce meaning ... the very concept of there being a single "full meaning" to be got to is thrown into question, and instead the interest is in looking at ways in which the text opens up and constructs possibilities of meaning, and how a reader is able to realise that meaning potential.* (Ray Misson, *Literary Theory*, VATE, 1994 p1)

The organising principle for the unit was Brian Moon's idea that readings generated in responding to a text may be categorised as:
1. Dominant
2. Alternative
3. Resistant.

In moving students towards resistant readings, in other words in introducing a critical literacy curriculum in the classroom, poetry must be responded to as a form of discourse, the governing conventions of which are embedded in historical and social contexts. In their questioning of the concept of a single 'full meaning', students begin also to challenge the manner in which dominant readings seek to present a 'naturalised' or 'common sense' view of the world. In this way, it is made obvious to students that reading, far from being a neutral activity, is complicit in the reproduction of social structures and relations.

> *One important function, therefore, for mainstream cultural texts of all kinds is to re-present and thus reinforce the dominant models of gender identity and behaviour. However, in such re-presentations there are often gaps, fissures – 'fault lines which the particular text will be concerned to render invisible by directing our attention to particular readings privileged and proffered by the text. An analysis of the text therefore ought first to identify the privileged reading held out by the text, and then to examine this reading and the text for what each fails to say, or struggles not to say.* (David Buchbinder, 'Reading the Masculine in *Strictly Ballroom*', in W Martino and C Cook (eds), **Gendered Texts**, (Adelaide: AATE, 1998).

Gender and gender relations have been an area much written about in studies of English curriculum and pedagogy in recent years. This unit draws on this work as, it seems to me, gender is an area of high relevance and great interest to adolescents.

Teaching Notes

These notes provide a guide to how the poems taught in this unit were introduced to students. The teaching/learning activities used in conjunction with each poem are outlined on the Students' pages.

1. *Late Fragment* – Raymond Carver

This poem was used to model for the students the close reading practices traditionally expected of students in the senior years. Such modelling shows students how, in reading a poem, notes may be made about such things as the language, the layout, and conventions which are used, as well as drawing their attention to the perception that the 'meaning' apparent in a poem may constitute a universal comment about life or human existence. The modelling of this process for students also highlights for them the opportunity such reading practice allows for the expression of a personal response to the poem.

In order to allow students to "experience" the poem before the model analysis was presented to them, the poem was read several times to the class and students were then allowed jot down their reactions and thoughts. These developing responses were shared with the class, generating a collective understanding. This provided a useful starting point for the students to then be able to evaluate their own developing progress as critical readers against the framework provided by my modelled analysis.

2. *Crossing the Bar* – Tennyson

The introduction of this poem, which has much in common with *Late Fragment* thematically as well as the context in which it was written and published, and the accompanying activity which asks students to compare the poems, immediately 'disrupted' the students' understanding of the reading of *Late Fragment* I had provided them with in my modelled analysis. This process of 'shifting the ground' and challenging the students' understanding allowed them to come to the realisation that the concept of a single, full meaning is a limiting one. Placing the poems side by side in this way allowed them to note in particular the differences between the Victorian Christian and late twentieth century secular sensibilities. This led into discussion of the 'modern consciousness' as operating in a godless universe, in which meaning resides for the individual in overcoming one's essential alienation by connecting with others, that is to say through one's relationships, rather than in the possibility of salvation through the grace of God.

Again, in order to promote student engagement with the poem, the poem was first read aloud a number of times and the students then had the opportunity to write down and share their initial reactions to the poem.

3. *To His Coy Mistress* – Andrew Marvell

Marvell's poem was introduced to students using an approach Ken Watson has called "Pupils as Questioners". (See David Mallick and Gill Jenkins (eds), **Poetry in the Classroom**, St Clair Press, 1983). In groups, having heard the poem read to them a number of times, students devised three or four questions about the poem they really wanted answered. These questions were pooled and then discussed. The students' understanding of the poem quickly began to develop as their questions were answered.

TEACHER'S PAGE

To extend the students' understanding of Marvell's language, Brian Moon's activity in which students order a paraphrasing of the first stanza, before paraphrasing the rest of the poem, proved to be useful. (See Moon, *Studying Poetry*, Chalkface Press, 1998, p36)

Students initially responded to the poem on an individual level by making the notes they would use for a critical analysis of the poem. These notes were used in a following lesson.

The 'Dominant Reading' activity for this poem was then introduced and contextualised for students by a brief overview of the nature of the English curriculum and teaching in schools and universities over the last decades. In particular the notion of a Cultural Heritage model of English as well as the nature and significance of Leavisite criticism was emphasised. The extract from the essay on the poem in *The Pelican Guide to English Literature* was then introduced and deconstructed by them.

4. *I Can't Feel the Sunshine* – Lesbia Harford

This lyric by an Australian poet and feminist neatly illustrates for students that when different texts are read 'side by side', new readings of both may be generated.

Lesbia Harford's name and her biographical details (see Drusilla Modjeska, ***The Poems of Lesbia Harford***, Sirius Books, 1955) were withheld from the students during their initial reading of the poem, after which they again jotted down their initial thoughts and reactions. The biographical details were not given to students until after they had completed the activity which required them to compare Harford's poem with Marvell's. Once these details were given to the students they were asked to reconsider their readings of both *To His Coy Mistress* and *I Can't Feel the Sunshine*.

Having reconsidered both poems, the students then looked at the binary oppositions created through the poems in their construction of gender roles and sexuality. This led to them generating a resistant reading of *To His Coy Mistress*, as outlined in the activity reproduced below. In the process of completing this activity students were, if only in a minor way, introduced to Queer theory, as it required them to adopt a gender or sexual position they would not normally read from.

5. Synthesis: Reading *To His Coy Mistress*

Students demonstrated their newly developed knowledge and skills in generating different readings of the same text by writing an essay which required them to outline a dominant, an alternative and a resistant reading of Marvell's poem, including an explanation of which reading they would privilege. This task draws on two outcomes in the New South Wales Advanced English Course for Years 11-12:

❖ A student explains and analyses the ways in which language forms and features, and structures of texts shape meaning and influence responses.

❖ A student analyses and synthesises information and ideas into sustained and logical argument for a range of purposes, audiences and contexts.

STUDENTS' PAGE

An Introduction to Literary Theory

Close Reading of a Poem – A Model

Biography/Background Details

Born in 1938, Carver came to prominence – and remains today best known – as a short story writer in the mid 1970s. Carver married early and this newfound recognition came after years of financial struggle as he worked in a series of low-paying jobs to support his family, only being able to write at night. Carver also experienced years of alcoholism, which was largely responsible for the failure of his marriage around the time that he began to achieve recognition as a writer. In 1977 he met the poet Tess Gallagher and they later married. Carver spent the last eleven years of his life with Gallagher. These years proved to be his most productive as a writer. In 1987 he was diagnosed with lung cancer, with the cancer quickly spreading to his brain. He died in 1988.

Late Fragment is the final poem in his final published collection, *A New Path to the Waterfall*, which was finished just weeks before his death and published posthumously in 1989.

Title may be read as a pun – 'late' and 'fragment' combine as in a last-minute idea, almost an afterthought, which is of little consequence. However, such modesty adds to the poignancy of the poem. 'Late' may also be read as Carver being conscious that this would be read after his death. 'Fragment' is, then, a deliberate downplaying of the weight and universality of the poem, which was his final word to the world.

past tense creates a sense of poignancy: finality and urgency.

Late Fragment

And did you get what
you wanted from this life, even so?
I did.
And what did you want?
To call myself beloved, to feel myself
beloved on the earth.

Beginning on conjunction creates a tone of intimacy, as if in the middle of a conversation. At the same time, the universality of the theme and subject matter indicates that Carver's poem is part of that ongoing dialogue as old as humankind: what is the meaning of life?

In either case, the conjunction creates an immediate sense of urgency: this question must be answered.

---

use of 2nd person initially suggests on one level that the poem is addressed to the reader, a personal connection between the poet and the reader is established, with the rhetorical question asking the reader to reflect on their own life. However, line 5 links 'you' and 'myself': this represents an internal dialogue, ie, the poet's inner voice. On another level, then, the poem represents the 'soul searching' of the poet, looking into himself, offering us what wisdom he can distil from a lifetime of experience.

The connections established between the reader and the poet – the way the poem operates on two levels – creates a **universality** of theme, giving a short poem great significance.

A declaration. Definite. Reflecting contentment, no regrets. At the same time, given the context in which it was written, this reflects incredible bravery.

Suggests a lot is remaining unsaid, buried in the past – a life of difficulties and disappointments. The poetic voice is imbued with realism, and as such, authority and wisdom. It also indicates that facing the end of life.

Deliberateness about the choice of the preposition "on" in the last line adds to the poignancy as he will soon be "in" the earth. At the same time, it reflects the humanist belief that there is no God and no after-life. Meaning in life comes from connecting with others during life, in loving and being loved.

Biography/Background Details

Alfred Tennyson was born in England in 1809. By the time of his death in October 1892 at the age of 83, he was a peer of the realm, the Poet Laureate, recognised as a spokesperson for the Victorian age, and that rarest of literary figures, a best-selling poet.

Tennyson was, in his lifetime, the object of extravagant hero-worship. The fact that he is the only poet ever to be elevated to the peerage (making him Lord Tennyson) for his work alone gives an indication of the regard in which he was held by Queen Victoria. She nominated his work as being her favourite literature, next to the *Bible*. Such was his fame that when he was travelling Tennyson had to wait until he was leaving to sign the register in hotels for fear of being mobbed.

Crossing the Bar was written on the back of an envelope in 1889 when he was 80, three years from his death. His son called it "the crown of your life's work" and Tennyson requested that it close each edition of his works.

Crossing the Bar

Alfred, Lord Tennyson

Sunset and evening star,
    And one clear call for me!
And may there be no moaning of the bar,
    When I put out to sea,

But such a tide as moving seems asleep,
    Too full for sound and foam,
When that which drew from out the boundless deep
    Turns again home.

Twilight and evening bell,
    And after that the dark!
And may there be no sadness of farewell,
    When I embark;

for tho' from out our bourne of Time and Place
    The flood may bear me far,
I hope to see my Pilot face to face
    When I have crost the bar.

Comparing Poems

Late Fragment and *Crossing the Bar* share in common the fact that they were the final poems in the last published works of two poets facing death. Both were intended to be the last word of the poets to the world.

Reading the poems side by side will inevitably influence the way that we read each on their own, in the process opening up new readings of each to us.

Consider the differences between the poems by completing the table below.

Late Fragment	Interpretation	*Crossing the Bar*	Interpretation
"to feel myself beloved on the earth"	Death is the end: there is no afterlife.	"When I have crost the bar"	Sea journey extended metaphor establishes that death marks the passing from life to afterlife.
"And did you get what you wanted from this life, even so?"		"And one clear call for me!"	A tone of excitement and expectation created by punctuation.
		"And may there be no sadness of farewell . . ."	Telling others how he wants them to feel and why.
"To call myself beloved, to feel myself beloved . . ."		"I hope to see my Pilot face to face . . ."	

1. Using this information, construct in pairs the notes you would use to write an **alternative** reading of *Late Fragment* to the **dominant** reading I have modelled for you.

2. Homework assignment: Using these notes as well as the work you have previously completed on *Crossing the Bar*, write a critical analysis of the poem of around 300-400 words (that is, 1-1½ A4 pages).

To His Coy Mistress

Andrew Marvell

Had we but world enough and time,
This coyness, lady, were no crime.   (coyness = coldness)
We would sit down and think which way
To walk, and pass our long love's day.
Thou by the Indian Ganges' side
Should'st rubies find; I by the tide
Of Humber would complain. I would
Love you ten years before the flood,
And you should, if you please, refuse
Till the conversion of the Jews.
My vegetable love should grow
Vaster than Empires and more slow;
An hundred years should go to praise
Thine eyes, and on thy forehead gaze;
Two hundred to adore each breast,
But thirty thousand to the rest;
An age at least to every part,
Adn the last age should show your heart.
For, lady, you deserve this state,   (state = stateliness, dignity)
Nor would I love at lower rate.
 But at my back I always hear
Time's winged chariot hurrying near;
And yonder all before us lie
Deserts of vast eternity.
Thy beauty shall no more be found;
Nor, in thy marble vault shall sound
My echoing song; then worms shall try
That long-preserved virginity,
And your quaint honour turn to dust,
And into ashes all my lust:
The grave's a fine and private place,
But none, I think, do there embrace.
 Now therefore, while the youthful hue
Sits on thy skin like morning dew,
And while thy willing soul transpires   (transpires = exhales)
At every pore with instant fires,
Now let us sport us while we may
And now, like amorous birds of prey
Rather at once our time devour
Than languish in his slow-chapped power.   (chapped = jawed)
Let us roll all our strength, and all
Our sweetness up into one ball,
And tear our pleasures with rough strife
Through the iron gates of life:
Thus, though we cannot make our sun
Stand still, yet we will make him run.

To His Coy Mistress – A Dominant Reading

Read the following text, which is adapted from an essay on the poetry of Andrew Marvell. The essay was 'The Poetry of Andrew Marvell' in B Ford (ed) *The Pelican Guide to English Literature Vol 3*).

Deconstruct the **values** and **ideas** which are represented in this reading of the poem by discussing the essay in your group and making notes in the boxes provided. Some examples have been completed for you.

> The use of paradox and exaggeration to produce an effect of comedy is one aspect of **the wit that is characteristic** of the poetry of Marvell. This quality of wit was inherited by Marvell from **his literary master Ben Jonson**. It pervades all of his best poetry, and is found in a particularly concentrated form in his love lyric *To His Coy Mistress*.
>
> The general idea on which the poem is based is **classical**: the belief in the virtue of enjoying oneself while one is still young (*'Carpe Diem'*) has been so often made the subject of lyric poetry as to be in some danger of becoming commonplace. Like Ben Jonson's *Song to Celia*, Marvell's *To His Coy Mistress* derives directly from the well-known **theme of the Latin poet Catullus, though** in its **details it is original.** The treatment of the theme is both witty and imaginative, the effect being gained, as **so often in Marvell, by the combination of rhythm and ambiguity:**
>
> > My vegetable love should grow
> > Vaster than empires, and more slow.
>
> 'Vegetable means 'having the power of sense-perception' as well as 'like a plant' (the Latin *vegetabilis* actually suggests speed and is equivalent to 'animating', 'enlivening', 'lively', 'quickening'). **The anti-climax is gained by the contrast between the size of the love and the time that it takes to grow, and rhythmically this is given in the verse by the sudden pause in the middle of the second line, and the three dead, heavy monosyllables, emphasised by the long-drawn-out vowels.** The reader taking 'vegetable' in the **Latin sense** would meet a sudden contradiction and reversal of meaning.

Boxes:
- Identifies what defines Marvell's poetry.
- Links Marvell to acknowledged great writers who have preceded him.

My Best Poetry Unit

The tone and movement of the verse both suddenly change in the second section of the poem, achieving the effect of surprise:

> But at my back I always hear
> Time's winged Chariot hurrying near: . . .

Then, pausing again, the poet concentrates the thought of death into a single brief and vivid image:

> Deserts of vast eternity.

The verse renders **perfectly the feeling** of desolation and the sense almost of betrayal that comes with death.

The epigrammatic force of this line and the reflections on the horrors of the tomb which follow it could be paralleled in many of Donne's lyrics where he contemplates this subject.

In *To His Coy Mistress*, Marvell treats this theme rather lightly. He is mainly concerned with death as a means of frightening his mistress and as a contrast with the invitation to love contained in the final section of the poem. **Vital and dynamic, love is contrasted with the coldness and silence of the tomb where the only movement is that of the worms, and with the dullness and monotony of a humdrum passive life,** the iron gates through which love must tear its way. **Time and death, the theme of so much Elizabethan and seventeenth-century poetry are conquered by love. The means by which the poet reaches this climax after the leisurely and apparently digressive opening is a triumph of control and organisation.** The verse gradually quickens, until at the end there is again a sudden pause, accentuating by contrast the momentum of the previous lines, giving the last two lines a note of finality.

> *Thus*, though we cannot make our Sun
> *Stand* still, yet we will make him run.

Follow Up Activity

This essay is representative of the cultural heritage model of the study of English. Discuss and answer the following questions with your group.

1. How does the cultural heritage model seek to establish the worth of a piece of literature?

2. What does it appear to value about the authors and the literature it encompasses?

3. What does it seem to put forward as the purpose(s) of literature?

4. How does it appear to construct meaning in literature?

5. In constructing this meaning, what does it appear to you to ignore?

6. From your own experience of studying English, what evidence can you find of the cultural heritage model in the curriculum?

Using the notes you have made above, attempt to reach a definition of the cultural heritage model in your group. After discussion, write your definition. Then discuss and list what your notes for a critical analysis of the poem both included and didn't include in comparison to this reading of the poem. To what extent, then, would you say your reading of the poem was a cultural heritage reading? How would you explain this?

My Best Poetry Unit

Biography/Background Details

Lesbia Harford (1891-1927), Australian poet and feminist, came of age during a turbulent period in Australian history. Overcoming a disrupted schooling, the consequence of her father's bankruptcy and eventual abandonment of his family, Harford graduated in law from Melbourne University in 1916; a notable feat in itself given that few women were practicing in the profession at this time. Her time at university proved to be a formative, radicalising influence on Harford as a writer. The movement for emancipation for women as well as the world wide socialist opposition to the First World War infused her subsequent work right up until her death with the twin sensibilities of social protest and the voicing of the experiences of women. Indeed Harford's commitment to political and social causes was such that, contrary to her mother's expectation that her degree would help regain for Harford the social standing that her father's aristocratic heritage had bestowed upon her as a young child, she did not go into legal practice. Rather she began work in textile and clothing factories and joined the International Workers of the World (IWW or 'Wobblies').

Harford's radicalism was as evident in her personal life as it was in her political activism. A proponent of free love, Harford lived with a series of lovers over many years. Her first serious affair was with a woman, Katie Lush, a philosophy tutor, with whom she fell deeply in love during her first year at University. The affair seems to have been brief, although their friendship endured, with Harford clearly noting in her lyric *I Can't Feel The Sunshine* the difficulty of maintaining a lesbian relationship in the conservative milieu of Melbourne University at that time. Another love was Guido Baracchi, like Harford a law student at Melbourne University and later a member of the IWW.

Harford lived her life with a heart condition, knowing that she was destined to die at a young age. She apparently did not expect to be widely published in her life time, with her brand of social protest and her concern with 'women's issues' failing to attract the attention of mainstream publishers for over half a century. It was not until the 1980s that her work was rediscovered.

(Source: Drusilla Modjeska, Introduction to *The Poems of Lesbia Harford*, Sirius Books, 1985.)

I Can't Feel the Sunshine

I can't feel the sunshine
Or see the stars aright
For thinking of her beauty
And her kisses bright.

She would let me kiss her
Once and not again.
Deeming soul essential,
Sense doth she disdain.

If I should once kiss her,
I would never rest
Till I had lain hour long
Pillowed on her breast.

Lying so, I'd tell her
Many a secret thing
God has whispered to me
When my soul took wing.

Would that I were Sappho,
Greece my land, not this!
There the noblest women,
When they loved, would kiss.

Comparing Poems

I Can't Feel the Sunshine and *To His Coy Mistress* share the form of a love lyric (a lyric being a short – or relative short – poem which expresses the thought and feelings of a single speaker in a personal and subjective fashion) and the theme of unrequited love.

Reading the poems side by side will inevitably influence the way that we read each on their own, in the process opening up new readings of each to us.

1. Consider the differences between the poems by completing the table below.

To His Coy Mistress	Interpretation	*I Can't Feel the Sunshine*	Interpretation
"Now therefore, ... now let us."	Persona is acting and in control.	"Would that I were Sappho ..."	Persona is acted upon and a victim of circumstances.
	Persona is able to openly express emotions/love.		
	Personal appeals to the loved one's rationality/intellect (ie, mind).	"Deeming soul essential ..."	Persona acknowledges must appeal to loved one's emotions.
	Persona is controlling and manipulative.		
"And tear our pleasures with rough strife ..."	Love is presented as physical and active.		Love is presented as sensual (ie, appeals richly to senses) and languorous (ie, a state of stillness or heaviness).
		"Lying so, I'd tell her Many a secret thing ..."	Love is presented as intimate and modest.
	Persona is brash and optimistic.		
	There is an element of fear in the relationship.		

2. The poem *I Can't Feel the Sunshine* will now be considered in the context of biographical details about the poet. How does this influence your reading of the poem?

3. Using this information, in pairs, construct the notes you would use to write an alternative reading of *To His Coy Mistress* to the dominant reading you have deconstructed in an earlier lesson.

To His Coy Mistress & *I Can't Feel the Sunshine*: Binary Oppositions

Working in pairs, use the notes you made when comparing the poems (keeping in mind how the brief biographical details of Lesbia Harford you were given opened up an alternative reading of *I Can't Feel the Sunshine*) to complete the following.

Heterosexuality (as represented in *To His Coy Mistress*)	Homosexuality (as represented in *I Can't Feel the Sunshine*)

Follow Up Activity

❖ Discuss the notes you have just made with your partner in order to develop a resistant reading of *To His Coy Mistress*. Then compose a paragraph which provides such a reading.

❖ This requires you to read the poem in terms of the way in which it may be said to confirm the patriarchy by naturalising a male dominated, exploitative model of heterosexuality.

❖ An interesting starting point for your discussion may be the following lines in the cultural heritage model essay: "In *To His Coy Mistress*, Marvell treats this theme (*Carpe Diem*) rather lightly. He is mainly concerned with death as a means of frightening his mistress . . ."

TEACHER'S PAGE

Sylvia Plath: A Discussion (Years 11-12) — Tim Lester

Teachers in Canada and the United Kingdom wishing to use this activity will have to make a couple of minor changes to the handout, which was designed for a Year 12 class in Sydney.

The text that the students were using was Sylvia Plath's *Ariel*. Almost any poems from *Ariel* would be appropriate, but certainly the following should be included:
Ariel,
Daddy,
The Applicant,
Kindness.

STUDENTS' PAGE

Sylvia Plath: A Discussion

Dear Arts Bloke

Your mission, and you **have** chosen to accept it, is to host a five minute segment of an Arts Show on ABC TV. You, as host, have been let down by the two academics who were going to be on a two-person panel as they have gone on a protest march about their pay deal.

Luckily, two carpark attendants have volunteered for the job as they have a passing interest in Plath's poems. They told me as they were polishing the Beemer. You have been given a couple of quotations from the writings of the two academics and, er, that's it.

You have an hour to prepare the segment, making sure that:

a) the attendants each "adopt" the character/viewpoint of one of the academics and use the actual quotation they have been given at some point;

b) you are able to introduce the participants and have discussed with them the direction the discussion will go and the key questions you are going to ask;

c) both you and the attendants are well-armed with evidence from the poems that will support your assertions;

d) the "show" will have the feel of an intelligent Arts Show (difficult, even for the ABC, ha).

Academic A – Professor Percy Hemroyd,
Chair of Reactionary Studies at Sydney University says, "The 'Feminist Movement' has hijacked these poems for their own use. Their true worth lies in their intensity and perfection of form." "Her finest poems are about our own fearfulness and vulnerability."

Academic B – Dr John Blabb,
Fellow of Beecroft University and author of *Daft Bitch: A History of Post-Colonial Genderings* says, "Plath's poetry was a brilliant and desperate attempt to locate what it was that hurt." "Her best work is an angry and effective portrait of essential male oppression at its darkest."

When it comes to filming, you may only use one side of the A4 cards provided. You have to make it look like these two jokers really are academics.

If you pull this off, I promise you a really nice office with a view next year. Promise.

Jonathan Slurr
Chief Executive
Australian Broadcasting Corporation

Part 2: Poets Speak

Introduction

The Birth of Poems

David Sutton

How anonymous, how uncircumstanced are their births.
One forgets they even happened, that at some point
In the workaday time of the world, clouds going by,
Hens in the yard, dogs barking, smoke on the wind,
There had to be a mothering, a making
Of words unmade: 'No longer mourn for me',
'Ah no, the years, the years!', 'Western wind,
When wilt thou blow?', 'So I did sit and eat'.

Yes, one is curious, but they are private
As births should be, hidden beyond recall
In the hollow places of time, in the folds of its silence,
Those lost hours, when the landscape of our love
Stayed as it was for a while: when clouds went by,
Hens scratched, dogs barked, and no-one knew at all,
Except for one who sat, his own sole witness,
Smiling at blank-eyed, inattentive air.

How Does A Poem Come About? (Years 9-12)
Roslyn Arnold

Roslyn Arnold, a Sydney poet, describes the genesis of her poem *Birdsong*, and suggests some questions for discussion. Her book of poems, *Mirror the Wind* (St Clair Press), was published in 1998.

Birdsong

Can a magpie sing a song so sweet
it cuts through sorrow
quickens the heartbeat?

Can that song come truly from a brain
so small and plainly formed
it knows no deflection
or regret like the sense of loss
when rose petals fall to the ground
nor complex thought
like the shape of futility
in measures of time
nor sorrow in the concept of yesterday's tomorrow

This pied bird hits the note truly every time
performs without applause
or any audience in sight
you'd swear its song
just landed on its head
like a fallen star
formed in another millennium
pitch black and pitch perfect

When fearful of desiring
another's wealth or fame
or overwhelmed by duties or fatigue
consolation swoops from the streaky sky
in this black velvet feathered dress
offering intervals of caramel smooth warbling
to liquefy concerns
about the nature of regret
and the wisdom of envying
with soft relief the performance of a bird

Background

It is sometimes hard to know just what makes one person express their feelings and creativity in a particular way. Some people love singing, some work with their hands, others love dancing or writing poetry. I never consciously set out to be a poet. That would have sounded very pretentious. I grew up in a family where books, reading and poetry were just part of normal life. My father loved poetry and could recite long verses from memory. He was very proud of the fact that he had acted as an altar boy in the New South Wales country town of Narrandera for the Catholic priest Father John Hartigan, who wrote poetry as John O'Brien. At school my introduction to poetry was Chaucer, Milton, Pope and Gerard Manley Hopkins. At university I read Blake, Wordsworth, Keats, Coleridge, W B Yeats. Ginsberg, Plath and so on. I guess I have read and taught a lot of poetry over the years. When I was studying poetry as part of a Masters of Arts degree, I decided I'd try writing poetry myself and I sent one of my first poems to The Sydney Morning Herald. I couldn't believe that they offered to publish it, and paid me $50. The experience gave me enough courage to feel I might continue to write poetry, but I would still feel cautious about claiming to be a poet. At the same time, I'd love to be a good poet.

I find that particular experiences, usually strongly emotional ones, attract me to writing poetry. I don't go out seeking the experience, it tends to just happen when I am in a contemplative frame of mind. There is a particular quality to the experience which claims my attention. It is hard to describe that quality except that it is familiar to me and has a special resonance – a combination of feeling and thought which I know I want to capture by finding the words to shape it. There is already some shape to the experience when I notice it, but the shape is rather lumpy and unformed. I want to take it in my hands and knead and mould it. You can see that the experience calls forth tactile and aural senses. While I am writing the poem I keep checking with that internal resonance to see whether it sounds right and looks right. I am sure that the experience I start with is quite tacit and unformulated when I begin. I think I actually create the experience as I go along, sometimes thinking it was inside me just waiting to happen. I think I actually have to make it happen by putting pen to paper. I still can't write poetry using a word processor. I have to start with a pen and my own handwriting.

I used to wonder whether poets set out to write for others, or just for themselves. I write initially just for myself but then I sometimes want to send the work out into the world, in trepidation.

I think I have probably taught myself to recognise that elusive quality of experience which calls to be shaped in poetry. I can ignore it, and often do, but I sometimes write a few notes to come back to later on. Probably like an artist who does preliminary sketches of a painting. I am sure that once you commit to expressing your experiences in a particular medium, you learn to notice things which help your cause. I notice words and rhythms of speech. I also notice nuances in voices.

STUDENTS' PAGE

I spent part of my childhood in Mildura, a Victorian country town bordering on the outback of New South Wales. We had birds as pets - an Eastern rosella, a galah, and a Major Mitchell cockatoo we were given as a fledgling. The family dog, Bozo, and that bird developed a special rapport. Bozo grieved noticeably when the bird became ill and died. I lost interest in birds once I went to boarding school in Melbourne. The interest was revived when I was in my mid-twenties and I discovered Rainbow lorikeets in the Pittwater area of Sydney. I bought a house in the area - my family said because of the birds - and they were right. I loved the fact that they were tame enough to eat out of your hands. I have written about feeding them in a poem called *Sunday Afternoon - Pittwater*. Rainbow lorikeets are richly coloured (emerald green, purple and red) but their call is very shrill, unlike the magpie, the subject of this poem.

I was working in the garden one afternoon when a magpie flew onto the lawn just outside the front gate and stood looking - well - transfixed. Suddenly, it broke into the most beautiful song and I just leant on my spade and listened. It just seemed the expected thing to do. Nothing would stop the magpie singing. Just when I thought the concert had ended it would start again, throwing its head back and looking to the sky. I guess I was struck by a number of thoughts and feelings. How can this small creature do so much with its 'bird's brain'? Who started all this? Why can't I express myself so effortlessly? Does it know how affecting its song is? Rather useless thoughts, but driven by very strong feelings of awe and even transcendence. I think transcendence is the feeling you have when something is so powerfully evocative you feel changed irrevocably. Once I had heard that magpie sing, I could no longer think of it as a simple, not particularly attractive, commonplace bird. I think these kinds of experiences are also spiritual - not in the church sense of spiritual- more in the sense of feeling very connected with something far beyond our knowing. I guess that is why I like the experiences which I write about as poems. They often make me feel there is something beautiful, purposeful and enduring about the world. That is a comforting thought when you face mortality.

I hope it is easy to see that I was inspired and moved by the bird's song. When we are moved to strong feelings like awe and wonder, we often think more deeply about things. That is what happened here. Don't worry if you cannot express easily in your own words what I am saying in this poem. Try instead to say how you feel when you read the lines. It is fine to say you feel a bit perplexed at some of the ideas like 'the shape of futility'. I can't put it into other words myself. It was a way of hinting at something ephemeral, uncatchable, difficult.

- There are words relating to music and drama in the poem. When you have noted them, suggest how they create a certain impression in the poem.

- What do you learn about the bird's physical appearance and skill from this poem? Is there anything more you would like to know?

- How would you describe the mood of the poem? Does it change?

- How would you describe the poet's feelings towards the bird?

❖ The poet describes the bird's song as 'intervals of caramel smooth warbling'. Does it work to combine the sense of taste with the sense of sound? Can you think of other phrases which could combine more than one sense? Poets and advertisers provide examples.

If you were to ask me what I most hope this poem would do for the reader, I'd say that I hope you find your own experiences which move you to express yourself in whatever way suits you. I'd also hope you might find unexpected sources of beauty in the world, including the joy of creating something for yourself, and maybe others, out of the resources of your own imagination.

Sunday Afternoon – Pittwater

The lorikeets feed noisily
dancing on skinny legs
like a cluster of articulated clowns
taking theatre to the trees

self-important, shrill and invincible
these birds enslave us all
in the glory of their stained glass colours

enthralled with being chosen
we fill their bowls
with bread and honey
savouring a different kind
of manna from heaven.

STUDENTS' PAGE

The Art of Light Verse (Years 8-12) – Tim Hopkins

Tim Hopkins lives in England. More of his verse can be found in another St Clair publication, *Imagined Corners.*

Great poetry moves us, but light verse should entertain. It must be fun. It must also be technically correct, formal in structure and readily understood. But it must not be doggerel, and distinguishes itself from worthless verse by its freshness and originality. Clichés, tired rhymes and ponderous diction are anathema to the form, and the best examples are characterised by wit, economy and panache. If readers feel they could have written the verse themselves it has failed: a display of expertise is part of the charm – the ideal might by Pope's "What oft was thought, but ne'er so well expressed".

Light verse has some first cousins, too. Nursery rhymes endure by virtue of their simple, exciting rhythms, rhymes and images. Even babies too young for language are beguiled by their insistent, incantatory charm. And adult song lyrics are a natural progression, with their greater intellectual and emotional appeal. So, whereas the Beatles' *She Loves You* would not qualify as light verse (lacking those virtues mentioned earlier), it is clear that Hart's *Bewitched, Bothered And Bewildered* and Sondheim's *Officer Krupke* are excellent examples of the form. The music gives an added dimension, but the texts are strong enough to stand alone.

Serious poetry and light verse sit very happily together. Eliot demonstrates this with *Prufrock* and *Macavity*. The former is the greater work, but we need smiles as well as tears. Light verse does not change lives as great poetry can, but it enriches them and should not be underestimated.

I cannot remember a time which I did not enjoy music, humour and the sound of words. Light verse contains a little of each passion and I was naturally drawn to it. My tendency to think to no purpose – unlike the other members of my scientific family – provided me with the necessary starting points. In *Who*, for example, I simply found myself fascinated by the notion of chiasmus, the inversion of word order in consecutive phrases/clauses. I spent days experimenting and simply listed those I thought worked best. *Parkbenchers* is not so much about the elderly, but the way western society tends to marginalise them. This was not a political poem, but merely a question: is this desirable?/fair? The comparison with Chinese society (say) may fill us with shame – or perhaps not.

Consequences is not an original theme. The way past, present and future are linked has been considered more profoundly by better minds than mine. I just felt impelled to express the idea in a short verse!

I enjoy paradoxes, and there is simple one at the heart of *Elementary*: endeavour without apparent success can reward us more richly than the wrong kind of success achieved too readily. I think this could be the basis for lively discussion: what is life **for**?

A recent survey in America revealed that the most popular creature on earth was the dog and the least popular, the cockroach. I'd go along with that, but the second placed domestic cat was only just edged out by the pooch, and in *Cat* I tried to celebrate its highly individual qualities. I sense this could lead quite easily to students attempting their own descriptions of a favourite animal. There can be few young people who don't feel strongly about animals, and strength of feeling often elicits most effective writing.

(In addition to the poems overleaf, some more verses by Tim Hopkins are to be found on page 97.)

Parkbenchers

We are the closed accounts,
The guests you don't announce,
The worked-out mines,
The discontinued lines.

We are the seized-up locks,
The stopped clocks,
The crumbling beams,
The frazzled seams.

We are the lives merely token,
The griefs unspoken,
The unheeded curses,
The unfollowed hearses.

Consequences

Everything the world has been
Informs the current way,
No need to brood about the past,
We live it every day.

Cat

Alluringly distant,
Seductively cool,
Disarmingly playful
But nobody's fool.

Endearingly wilful,
Aloof from the crowd,
Bewitchingly haughty
And famously proud.

This lovable tyrant
Beguiles and unnerves
And makes of his master
A minion who serves

Elementary

Everything King Midas touched
Would turn at once to gold,
And when he touched his daughter,
She too fell still and cold.

He'd lost the girl he treasured,
The child he longed to hold,
Whose life was far more precious
Than palaces of gold.

The alchemist had no such power –
The opposite, in fact –
The magic touch King Midas had
Demonstrably he lacked.

For every mix and treatment,
In crucible and mould,
Belied his wayward theories,
And would not turn to gold.

But energy and hope remained,
His failure's ghost to lay,
As self-belief and cheerfulness
Drove doubt and gloom away.

Two seekers for this element,
And only one made gold,
Which caused the worst disaster
A father could behold.

Yet strangely, for the alchemist,
A better tale is told –
Of happiness – though what he touched
Would never turn to gold.

Who

Who despairs of content may be content with despair;
Who lives in hope must hope to live,
Who is friend to all is not all friend;
Who boasts of honour may not honour the boast;
Who assumes he is correct cannot correct what he assumes;
Who has a wealth of love will have no love of wealth.

STUDENTS' PAGE

Remembering Childhood – Carl Leggo

Carl Leggo is a Canadian poet who grew up in Newfoundland. He writes:

"I wrote the poem *Growing Up Perpendicular on the Side of a Hill* about ten years ago. This summer I returned to the neighbourhood where I grew up, my first visit in over four years. Almost everything has changed. Almost everybody I knew as a boy has died or moved. Many houses, including my parents' home, have been destroyed as part of an extensive urban redevelopment project. And, yet, in my memory's eye, I saw the old neighbourhood, vibrant and vivid and vital, almost as if I was watching a film. In my poetry I store the memories of family and neighbours; I record the stories of ordinary people, and I know the extraordinariness of their lives. I seek to honour the people I grew up with, even when the stories are hilarious or horrible. Above all, their stories haunt me, and I want to hallow their memories.

"In *Pedagogy of the Heart*, published posthumously in 1997, Paulo Freire acknowledges from the perspective of a long life nearing its end that his childhood backyard was a space connected to many spaces. Freire writes: 'My childhood backyard has been unveiling itself to many other spaces – spaces that are not necessarily other yards. Spaces where this man of today sees the child of yesterday in himself and learns to see better what he had seen before. To see again what had already been seen before always implies seeing angles that were not perceived before. Thus, a posterior view of the world can be done in a more critical, less naive, and more rigorous way.' Freire encourages me that 'the more rooted I am in my location, the more I extend myself to other places so as to become a citizen of the world. No one becomes local from a universal location.'

"I encourage all of us to pay attention to our own backyards, the people and places that shape us. To write our own stories is to explore the heart with its rhythms and energies and emotions; to write our own stories is to communicate and connect with the stories and the hearts of others."

Growing Up Perpendicular on the Side of a Hill

in a house hammered into a hill hanging over the Humber Arm I grew up and watched the cargo ships come and go without me through spring summer autumn winter and watched Ro Carter open the shutters on his store where everything you ever needed could be bought and listened for the mill steam whistle announcing the hours and disasters always whistling

and at sixteen I left 7 Lynch's Lane Corner Brook Newfoundland and I've been leaving for more than two decades never staying anywhere long enough to get to know people well enough to have a fight an argument even and perhaps all this time I've been running away from Lynch's Lane where I lived a soap opera with no commercial breaks and grew up perpendicular on the side of a hill

with Gordie Gorman whose mother one Christmas gave him a hunting knife with a blade like a silver bell but Gordie Gorman refused to carve the turkey and hunted through the house with one clean slice down to the side cut off his penis instead and was rushed to Montreal where it was sewed back on though neighbours said it never worked right again and Gordie Gorman said only I wanted to see how sharp it was

and Francie Baker who spent a whole year in bed just woke up on New Year's Day and said I'm not getting up this year and day after day just lay in bed reading the newspaper and looking out the window and she always waved at Cec Frazer Macky my brother and me when we climbed the crab tree to watch her

and Tommy Struckless the midget who we all gave nickels to do hand-stands and somersaults and was fierce and cranky like a crackie dog and ran off to Toronto and became a wrestler

and Frankie Sheppard who disappeared during his high school graduation and was found three days later in the trees near Wild Cove mute with the stories aswirl around his head LSD and Old Niagara and rock music and his girlfriend's mother finding him pinched between her daughter's legs like a lobster

and Mikey Bishop who stopped everybody on the road flashed open his black overcoat never without it want to buy a watch hundreds of watches pinned to the inside of the coat the only thing ticking about Mikey Bishop said Cec

and Bonnie Winsor who rubbed herself with coconut oil and lay on a red blanket in her underwear like a movie star between sheets of tin foil toasting in the spring sun and sometimes smiled at Cec Frazer Macky my brother and me hiding in the tall grass watching her turning and cooking like a chicken on a spit and we asked her if we could take Polaroid snaps and she said yes but by the time we saved up enough money for film summer was over and Bonnie Winsor's brown body was hidden away for another year

and Bertie Snooks who joined the army got a haircut flew to Cornwallis and was run over by a sergeant in a jeep without meeting the enemy even before he completed basic training

and Sissy Fudge who was the smartest girl in Harbourview Academy and could have been a lawyer or doctor or engineer but had her first baby at fifteen and almost one a year for the next decade or two like a friggin' Coke machine said Macky

and Janie Berkshire who built a big two-storey house with her husband Pleaman and the night Cec Frazer Macky my brother and I carried and dragged Pleaman all the way up Old Humber Road and Lynch's Lane from the Caribou Tavern where

he sometimes went after prayer meetings at the Glad Tidings Tabernacle Janie Berkshire threw Pleaman out the new plate glass window and he fell two storeys buried in snow and Cec Frazer Macky my brother and I hid Pleaman in Cec's basement for the night and Janie Berkshire painted the house magenta and raised three daughters and served tea and walnut sandwiches at weekly meetings with the women of Lynch's Lane but wouldn't let Pleaman Berkshire or any other man in the house again

and Denney Winsor whose wife ran off with an
optometrist and Denney started lifting weights
in order to beat the shit out of the
optometrist but enjoyed weightlifting so much
he shaved all the hair off his legs and chest
and came third in the Mr Corner Brook
Bodybuilding Contest

and Sammy Sheppard who turned sixteen and
didn't want to be a boy scout or a missionary
or an honours student or a star basketball
player and took his father's lead mallet and
smashed up seven of the concrete benches at
Margaret Bowater Park until he couldn't lift
the mallet over his head anymore and spent a
few weeks in the Whitburne Detention and
Reform Center for Juveniles where he was a
model inmate

and Louella Skiffington who always wore her
fuchsia dress to the Glad Tidings Tabernacle
every Sunday and Wednesday night and for
special prayer meetings I'm devoted to the
soul-saving business she said until she came

home early one night ill and found Ronnie
Skiffington singing hymns with Amanda Parsons
the choir director and Louella stopped wearing
her fuchsia dress stopped going to the Glad Tidings
Tabernacle parked her old life like a
car wreck in the backyard and most nights
brought Greek and Portuguese second mates home
from the Caribou Tavern still saving souls the
neighbours said

but for all my running away I never escape
Lynch's Lane like the weather always mad
spring under a moon always full bonfire summer
autumn ablaze winter without end the hill
where I grew up perpendicular

Teaching Suggestions: 'Growing Up Perpendicular' (Years 10-12) – Joe Belanger & Glenys Acland

Introduction

Childhood memories frequently provide authors with material for their literary works, despite disclaimers that "all characters are purely fictional and do not depict any person living or dead", a clause written partly in response to the widespread delusion that this might forestall costly lawsuits. Leggo makes no such claim: his characters are his boyhood friends, neighbours and townspeople and their stories are of the joys, wrangles, and frustrations of daily living in a town where anybody's business is everybody's business. Much of our interest in *Growing Up Perpendicular...* is in what the author calls the "soap opera" quality of his life: gossip about love, hate, infatuation, self-mutilation, drugs, prayer meetings, and, of course, adultery.

One way to introduce the poem is to discuss soap operas: what stories do they tell? why do they hold our attention? Of course, danger lurks in exploring connections with students' lives: town gossip and school gossip might be the source of unnecessary embarrassment.

The poem also explores social class, particularly, as Leggo notes, from a Marxist perspective. Consequently, an exploration of students' notions of social class may help them to prepare for the poem. What are the dominant attitudes toward the concept of social class in their own country? How do those attitudes match reality? What are some ways of moving up in the world?

Activities

1. **The title of the poem**
   What attracts students to the title? What does "perpendicular" suggest? How does this play out in the poem? Substitute words for "perpendicular" which would provide a more bland (eg, "happily" or "contented") introduction to the poem; or words which would give a more emotional connotation (eg, "a loser" or "a poet") or words with a sharper focus (eg, "out of kilter" or "in a soap opera"). If you have discovered words which you think would improve the title, justify them in terms of the poem. In any case, use the poem to describe how the poet has grown up "perpendicular".

2. **The structure of the poem**
   Describe globally the structure of the poem (eg, after the first two stanzas which set up the poem, each stanza presents one vignette; most stanzas begin with "and" followed by a person's first and last names and "who". What does "but" signal at the beginning of the final stanza? Most stanzas are seven to nine lines long, the poem is completely without punctuation, capitalisation is reserved for proper nouns but not used at the beginning of any sentence or line – what effects are achieved by these literary devices? The class might also investigate the effects of the order that the vignettes are presented in (eg, if the poem were physically cut into stanzas, would students put it back together in the same order? How would they justify their choices?).

3. **Humour**
   One of the most rewarding explorations students might undertake is to examine the humour in the poem which is derived in a number of ways. Of course, the stories themselves are humorous (eg, Francie Baker who said "I'm not getting up this year" [and the boys climbing the crab tree to watch her lie in bed]). But the expression and language Leggo uses are also important contributors to the humour. Many stanzas end with an observation, frequently a droll comment by one of the poet's friends (eg, "the only thing ticking about Mikey Bishop said Cec" or "still saving souls the neighbours said").

TEACHER'S PAGE

Others end with apparently naive comments (eg, "said only I wanted to see how sharp it was" or "Bonnie Windsor's brown body was hidden away for another year"). The narrator's reports of community gossip (eg, "though neighbours said it never worked right again") provides humour too. Students might make a list of such comments and use it to discuss the ways that the author tickles our fancies. What effect does the humour give to the pathos and shocking events in the poem?

4. **Themes**
   It is worth exploring the threads which run through the vignettes (eg, religion, sex, betrayal, joy, wonder, simplicity). One way to do this is to make a two or three word title for each stanza and then begin with a discussion of the importance of the first (Gordie Gorman) and final (Louella Skiffington) vignettes. For example, the first vignette deals with self-mutilation and the final vignette explores adultery and retribution. What are the next most powerful vignettes and why are they place din the poem as they are?

5. The narrator is clearly an adult looking back on snapshots from his childhood ("at sixteen I left . . . and I've been leaving for more than two decades"). We can expect, then, that much of the detail surrounding the events has been forgotten and that the author has focused on the important human understandings that the events illustrate. If that were not so, very few people in other areas of the world would be interested in the events in Corner Brook, Newfoundland. Small groups of students might explore what they feel to be one or two of the most interesting insights about human nature they discovered in the poem and share these observations with the rest of the class.

6. In *Teaching to Wonder*, his book on teaching poetry, Carl Leggo suggests that this poem reflects the Marxist view that citizens must learn to interrogate class constructs. It might be worth exploring such concepts as "old money", "caste", and "social mobility" with students and using the concepts to discuss ways the poem challenges beliefs underlying social class.

7. The narrator describes himself as "living a soap opera with no commercial breaks". Using evidence from the poem, students might discuss how life as depicted in the poem might be considered a soap opera. How does it compare with the soaps on TV?

Writing Opportunities

Growing Up Perpendicular ... invites sequels. Students might analyse the structure of one of the vignettes and use it as a basis to write a vignette about their neighbourhoods (or, to play it safe, a television show or a published short story). They might then write the vignette in another verse form (say rhyming couplets or a sonnet) and compare the effects of each verse form.

The vignettes also lend themselves to visual presentation as comic strips. Each story has a beginning, middle, and end which could be the subject of a three or four frame comic strip. Use one vignette from the poem as the basis for a short story. Consider the details you would need to add to write three or four thousand words on the vignette and the ways you would keep your reader's attention.

Art Activity

Growing Up Perpendicular ... is startling in its realistic presentation of life in a small town. The poem lends to an abstract visual art representation: drawings and shapes cut out to create a collage.

Part 3: Some Additional Poetry Units

Teacher's Page

Playing with Language (Years 7-10) — Ken Watson

Beheadings (Miroslav Holub)

Initially, let the students, in groups, try to work out what is happening in this poem (which is a series of riddles). It is likely that one group will tumble to the fact that if one 'beheads' the word 'black' (a colour), one ends up with the word 'lack'.

Here are the answers to the others

2. m/arrow 3. g/lance 4. g/lobe 5. p/rice 6. s/lumber 7. s/cent 8. s/pine

Once the groups have solved the riddles, they can create their own 'Beheadings' poems. (They should start by making a list of words that can be 'beheaded', e.g. 'brain', 'sport'.)

Riddles

1. A pair of spectacles

2. A wheelbarrow

3. A piano

4. Egg

After solving these in their group, the students can be asked to write their own, either individually or as a group activity. As Sandy Brownjohn points out in her book ***Does It Have to Rhyme?*** (London: Hodder, 1980. Pp.35-6),

> *One of the benefits of asking children to write riddles is that, since they are not allowed to mention the subject, they are forced to think harder about it. They must choose their words carefully so as not to make it too easy to guess, and they must search out the hidden aspects of their subject, thus looking at it more closely than they ever have before. Being able to find other ways of expressing what might be a commonplace object will be of great value later on in other poems.*

[Sandy Brownjohn's two books on teaching children to write poetry - the second is ***What Rhymes with 'Secret'?*** (London: Hodder, 1982) - are an invaluable teacher reference.]

Three verses by Tim Hopkins

All three of these pieces lend themselves to imitation; for example, *Secret Message* can lead to an exploration of the possibilities of homophones, and *Shakespeare* to playing with anagrams. Sometimes, anagrams can prove surprisingly apt: Adolf Hitler becomes 'Hated for ill', and Florence Nightingale 'Flit on, cheering angel!'.

Parody (Years 8-11)

Parody imitates the writing of others in such a way as to make the style or tone or ideas seem ridiculous. The method employed usually involves exaggeration. The trochaic metre employed by Longfellow in his long narrative *Hiawatha* has struck many readers as inappropriate, as a long succession of trochaic tetrameters creates a monotonous, sing-song effect. This, together with Longfellow's fondness for irritating repetition, has made *Hiawatha* the butt of many parodies. An excellent collection of parodies, both verse and prose, is **Imitations of Immortality**, edited by E O Parrott (Harmondsworth: Penguin, 1987). A parody of Richard Lovelace's poem, *To Lucasta, Going to the Warres*, is on p123.

Pastiche (Years 9-12)

Alison Pryde's *Sonnet in the Words of Shakespeare* is a very clever example of pastiche, which provides an entertaining activity to end a unit on a Shakespeare play or a unit where a number of poems by the one author have been studied. For example, Mark McFadden, in his **The Course of True Love: A Workshop Approach to A Midsummer Night's Dream** (Sydney: St Clair Press), suggests that the students, in groups, arrange lines from the play dealing with love into a poem entitled *The Course of True Love Never Did Run Smooth*.

If a senior class is studying a group of Shakespeare's sonnets, be sure to include Sonnet XVIII (*Shall I campare thee to a summer's day?*). After the pastiche activity has been completed, draw the class's attention to a curious fact: if the lines of this sonnet are read in reverse order, ending with the question, the sonnet still, with minor alterations to the punctuation, makes perfect sense. This is also true of one or two others of Shakespeare's sonnets.

Playing With Language

Beheadings

Miroslav Holub

Behead a colour,
and find a shortage.

Behead a vegetable,
and find a missile.

Behead a look,
and find a weapon.

Behead a sphere
and find part of your ear.

Behead the cost,
and find something to eat.

Behead sleep,
and find rubbish.

Behead a smell,
and find a coin.

Behead a backbone,
and find a tree.

Riddles

1. Without a bridle,
   Or a saddle,
   Across a thing
   I ride a-straddle,
   And those I ride,
   By help of me,
   Though almost blind,
   Are made to see.

   Anon.

2. No mouth, no eyes
   Nor yet a nose.
   Two arms, two feet,
   And as it goes,
   The feet don't touch the ground,
   But all the way,
   The head runs round.

   Anon.

3. I stand on legs but do not walk,
   I make clear sounds but do not talk.
   I keep to time without a clock
   No key of mine can open locks.
   I'll play all day, but never shirk
   If I have hands to make me work.

   Barrie Wade

4. In marble halls as white as milk,
   Lined with a skin as soft as silk,
   Within a fountain crystal-clear,
   A golden apple doth appear.
   No doors there are to this stronghold,
   Yet thieves break in and steal the gold.

   Traditional

Secret Message

Tim Hopkins

I'm fonder view,
A door ewe,
Were ship ewe,
Add mire ewe;
My art beat sly Kenny thing.

Shakespeare

Tim Hopkins

SEEK A PHRASE
SEE A SPARK, EH?
AH, SPEAK, SEER!
HE'S ERA'S PEAK.

Elusive

Tim Hopkins

Solomon Grundy,
Bjorn on a Monday,
Kristin, Tuesday
Marit, Wednesday
Al on Thursday
Wes on Friday
Dai on Saturday
Barrett, Sunday –
Quite a conman, Suleman
Gründig.

Hiawatha (Excerpt)

Henry Wadsworth Longfellow

Out of childhood into manhood
Now had grown my Hiawatha,
Skilled in all the craft of hunters,
Learned in all the lore of old men,
In all youthful sports and pastimes,
In all manly arts and labours.

Swift of foot was Hiawatha;
He could shoot an arrow from him,
And run forward with such fleetness,
That the arrow fell behind him!
Strong of arm was Hiawatha,
He could shoot ten arrows upward,
Shoot them with such strength and swiftness,
That the tenth had left the tow-string
Ere the first to earth had fallen!

He had mittens, Minjekahwun,
Magic mittens made of deerskin;
When upon his hands he wore them,
He could smite the rocks asunder,
He could grind them into powder.
He had moccasins enchanted,
Magic moccasins of deerskin;
When he bound them round his ankles,
When upon his feet he tied them,
At each stride a mile he measured!

The Modern Hiawatha

George A Strong

He killed the noble Mudjokivis.
Of the skin he made him mittens,
Made them with the fur side inside,
Made them with the skin side outside.
He, to get the warm side inside,
Put the inside skin side outside;
He, to get the cold side outside,
Put the warm side fur side inside,
That's why he put the fur side inside,
Why he put the skin side outside,
Why he turned them inside outside.

Coochi-Coochi

Bill Greenwell

By the supermarket trolley,
In an eezi-fold-up buggy,
Underneath a quilto-kumfi
Lay the sacred infant dribbling,
And he spoke the tongue of tinies,
Sang the tongue of Not-Yet-Toddler,
"Oba-gurgle, oogle-oo-goo,
Bubba-dubba, mummee-wah-wah,
Urkle-gobba, plugga-wagga,
Blubbli-obblah!" wailed the infant
'Til his mummee, Mrs. Buncer,
Plugged his cakehole with a dummee,
Dummee dipped in maple syrup,
As approached a gushing grannee.

Grannee exited from Tesco,
From the quik-food in the freezer,
Looked into the fold-up buggee,
Whispered "Coochi-mudjekeewis,
Husa-booti fula-babba,
Izzaneetha spitta-dadda,"
Called him "Coochi-mudjekeewis,"
Even though his name was Jason
(Full name Jason Kristin Buncer),
He who plucked away his dummee,
Blew the sacred wind upon her,
Sicked upon the avocado
In the Tesco bag of grannee.

Sonnet in the Words of Shakespeare

Alison Pryde

Now entertain conjecture of a time
In a New Zealand spring. No rough winds shake
The darling buds of May or violets dim.
The isle is full of birdsong and sweet airs
And sunlight sparkles on the southern seas,
Smooth waters for the shallow bauble boats.
And I, like Patience on a monument,
Smiling at grief, sit on a bank whereon
The wild thyme blows and where the bee sucks,
Here, in a lemon grove in Arcady.
Men close their doors against a setting sun
And finished now are all my dancing days.
I'll leave this garden, larded with sweet flowers,
And girdle half the earth in twenty hours.

TEACHER'S PAGE

What is a Poem? (Years 7-9) — Glenys Acland & Joe Belanger

Introduction

What is a poem? Does a poem require metre? rhythm? rhyme? Must it be musical? Does it explore eternal truths? Is the language complex? Is figurative language required? Does it evoke visual or emotional responses from the audience? Can it simply explore an insight? Boswell and Nowlan chose two very different subjects (a phenomenon of nature and a team sport) as the topics of their poems, but the poems have a number of features in common. Students might use these similarities and differences along with characteristics of other poems they are familiar with to address the question "What is a poem?"

Suggested Activities and Questions

1. Boswell's work might be described as a sentence which lacks a finite verb. Cite evidence to support the premise that it is more than a simple sentence. Such evidence might include the language used to express the ideas, the clever use of words and ideas to create a mental image, and suggestions that the poem goes beyond its literal meaning.

2. How important is the title, *Shadows*, to our understanding of the poem? Would reading the poem without knowing the title provide more delight in discovery than reading it with the title?

3. Good poetry frequently helps us to look at ideas and objects in new ways. Describe ways in which this poem might cause us to look at shadows in new ways.

4. What picture does Nowlan paint of an ice hockey player? If you know nothing about ice hockey, how might you describe the game and the players? What are the players' attitudes? What is the level of violence involved in the game?

5. In what way does stanza three set the reader up for stanza four? The first three metaphors that Nowlan uses are of wild, animate creatures: a gull, a tiger, and a peacock. The fourth, however, is an inanimate object and changes the entire picture: a wind-beaten tree. Are you able to visualise the tree "getting up" as easily as you are the gull circling, the tiger charging, or the peacock strutting? What is the effect of this difference? Does the tree get up more slowly, for example?

6. Nowlan chose to begin each of the four sentences which comprise *Hockey Player* with the same word: "like". Describe the effect of this strategy. "Like", of course, is the marker of a simile; what are the strengths and weaknesses of similes? How are these reflected in the poem?

7. Write a poem about another sport which gives the reader both the flavour of the sport and the attitudes of the players. List ten words not found in Nowlan's poem which could describe his hockey player (eg, graceful, agile) and apply them to your sport. You might want to follow the structure of Nowlan's poem and make each stanza a simile beginning with "Like".

What is a Poem?

Shadows

Gary Boswell

> Pictures
> painted by
> the
> sun
>
> rubbed
> out
> by
> the
> clouds.

Hockey Player

Michael Nowlan

Like a gull
he circles.

Like a tiger
he charges.

Like a peacock
he struts.

Like a wind-beaten tree
he gets up
from a bone-crushing
check into the boards.

Changing the Point of View (Years 9-12)
Trevor Gambell & Sam Robinson

The Doctor

Gary Hyland

No more boxers for me.

Bar room brawlers,
that's another story.
They don't train
to destroy people.
No one pays to watch
a couple of drunks
demolish furniture.

Four and a half hours
inside this kid's head
and *I'll* fight anyone
who calls this *sport*.

Prize fighting?
You want to know
this kid's prize?
Bifrontal craniotomy,
three subdural haematomas,
possible embolisms
possible skull fracture,
total left hemiplegia.

Let me translate.
If he ever wakes up
half life in the cabbage patch,
maybe complete loss
of his whole left side,
years of therapy
so he can shuffle,
drool and gawk about.

No more boxers for me.
I'm a neurosurgeon
not a bloody botanist.

The male speaker of this poem is a doctor treating a prize fighter. Rewrite this poem from the point of view of the prize fighter or one of these people: the prize fighter's girlfriend, wife, coach, mother, or father. When you talk afterwards about your poem, think about both what you said in your poem, and the issues and concerns you faced while writing it.

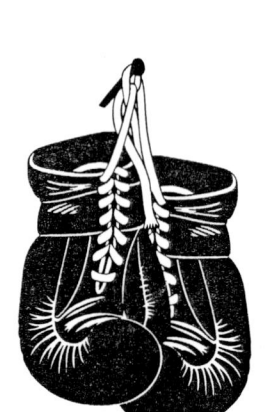

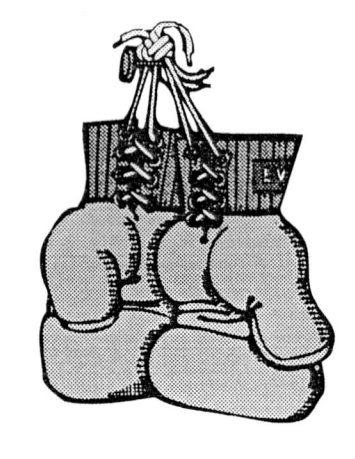

Teaching *The Forsaken* (Years 10-12) – Joe Belanger

Introduction

Modern societies have evolved complex ways to assist and support citizens who are unable to fend for themselves. We have a variety of social programs ranging from government-sponsored Medicare to welfare and food banks. Much of our ability to support others through welfare, however, is dependent upon the affluence of society. Students might speculate on how societies which have few resources at their disposal support and care for the old and the weak. If they lived a nomadic life on a desert, constantly moving in search of food and water, or in tribes in the Arctic, following the migrations of the caribou herds to keep near a food supply, how would they support the less fortunate in their midst?

The activities below suggest two approaches to *The Forsaken*: a guided reader-response approach which integrates reading, writing, speaking and listening to help students arrive at their own interpretations of the poem; and more traditional questions and activities which are prompts to explore the poem. To understand poetry, Frederico Garcia Lorca noted, "we need four white walls and silence where the poet's voice can weep and sing".

A Guided Reader-Response Approach

This poem lends itself to a guided response (Rudi Engbrecht, based on the work of Patrick Dias). The steps include:

1. Students read the poem to themselves silently (either in class at the end of a lesson or at home) and write a short response in their learning logs.

2. When students return to class, they are given a few minutes to read their responses to the poem and then make revisions or additions to the initial responses.

3. Students meet in groups of about five to discuss their responses. Teacher appoints a chair and a recorder; the crucial factor is that each student shares one response before anyone in the group is allowed to comment. Once each student has presented one idea, the chair calls for volunteers to comment. The teacher monitors each group and decides when to move to the next stage. Usually a maximum of fifteen minutes is allotted to this stage.

4. Students return to their learning journals and make any additions or revisions appropriate.

5. Groups re-form to discuss which ideas the chair will present to the plenary group. This stage generally takes no more than five minutes.

6. The plenary session provides an opportunity for each group to share its deliberations with other members of the class. The teacher chairs this session and asks each chair to present one or two ideas in turn. Then the teacher keeps a list of class members who wish to respond. If conversation flags, the teacher might offer a question or two, but Engbrecht feels that this might encourage students to wait to find out what the teacher really wants. Engbrecht opposes any summary by the teacher for the same reason.

7. Students return to their journals and make additions or revisions in light of the class discussion.

TEACHER'S PAGE

Additional Approaches

Teachers not using the Engbrecht approach might be interested in some of the following questions and activities:

1. Prereading discussion: What happens to the old and infirm in our culture? What shapes our attitudes toward these practices?

2. Exploring the poem. What connotations do students have of "forsaken"? Do students consider the Chippewa woman to be "forsaken"? List other words which might be used to describe her. Is there a contrast in the language which describes the Chippewa woman in part I and part II of the poem?.

3. Sacrifice. The plots of the two vignettes in the poem should not be difficult for students to understand; however, they may be more willing to accept the sacrifices she makes so that she and her son can live in the first part of the poem than they are to accept her sacrifice so that her tribe can survive in the second part. What evidence is there in the poem to suggest that the Chippewa woman was not the first of her people to be left behind?

   Although the title of the poem is *The Forsaken* with its connotations of abandonment and betrayal, the Chippewa woman appears to die with dignity. Indeed, she is described as being "valiant" and "unshaken". Students should locate evidence in the poem to support generalisations about the author's attitudes to the Chippewa woman's choice.

4. In the first section of the poem, the Chippewa woman fights against all odds to keep life. This may be seen as a natural response, especially in an environment where death is always just a few steps away. In the end, this natural process continues: she dies with dignity when she can no longer help her society to stay one step ahead of death. Early in the poem her duty was to live; in the end it was to die. What are our obligations in today's society? Do we ever have an obligation to sacrifice our lives for the good of our fellow citizens?

5. The art of the storyteller. Scott begins his poem in the middle of a snowstorm out on a lake. The Chippewa woman's situation is critical and we are absorbed in her sacrifices and her will to live. Consequently, we do not ask such questions as "What is a woman with a sick child doing on a lake in the last hours of a great storm far from the Fort?" "What disregard for her life and the life of her baby put her in this position?"

   Part II of the poem also leaves major questions unanswered as Campbell focuses on the emotional highlight. Students might raise questions such as: "Why did the tribe choose this time to abandon her?" and "Why does she just sit there and wait to die?" How does ignoring such questions help the poem to achieve its effect?

6. Beyond the poem. Writing assignments which grow out of *The Forsaken* include vignettes which contrast sacrifices people have made early in life for the good of society (veterans of wars, for example) with their treatment by their governments in later years. Alternatively, students might write a movie script for a documentary about the Chippewa woman's life, or more broadly, life in any very hostile environment.

7. The concept of euthanasia is guaranteed to spark a good deal of heated debate. To distance students from the personal revelations which such a debate might bring out, such activities as preparing posters, news reports, or political speeches from a range of perspectives (eg, right-to-die groups, groups which oppose euthanasia) might be considered.

The Forsaken
Duncan Campbell Scott

I

Once in the winter
Out on a lake
In the heart of the north-land,
Far from the Fort
And far from the hunters,
A Chippewa woman
With her sick baby,
Crouched in the last hours
Of a great storm.
Frozen and hungry,
She fished through the ice
With a line of the twisted
Bark of the cedar,
And a rabbit-bone hook
Polished and barbed;
Fished with the bare hook
All through the wild day,
Fished and caught nothing;
While the young chieftain
Tugged at her breasts,
Or slept in the lacing
Of the warm tikanagan.
All the lake-surface
Streamed with the hissing
Of millions of ice flakes
Hurled by the wind;
Behind her the round
Of a lonely island
Roared like a fire
With the voice of the storm
In the deeps of the cedars.
Valiant, unshaken,
She took of her own flesh,
Baited the fish-hook,
Drew in a grey-trout
Drew in his fellows,
Heaped them beside her,
Dead in the snow.
Valiant, unshaken,
She faced the long distance,
Wolf-haunted and lonely,
Sure of her goal
And the life of her dear one:
Tramped for two days,
On the third in the morning,
Saw the strong bulk
Of the Fort by the river,
Saw the wood-smoke
Hang soft in the spruces,
Heard the keen yelp
Of the ravenous huskies
Fighting for whitefish:
Then she had rest.

II

Years and years after,
When she was old and withered,
When her son was an old man
And his children filled with vigour,
They came in their northern tour on the verge of winter,
To an island in a lonely lake.
There one night they camped, and on the morrow
Gathered their kettles and birch-bark,
Their rabbit-skin robes and the mink-traps,
Launched their canoes and slunk away through the islands,
Left her alone forever,
Without a word of farewell,
Because she was old and useless,
Like a paddle broken and warped,
Or a pole that was splintered.
Then, without a sigh,
Valiant, unshaken,
She smoothed her dark locks under her kerchief,
Composed her shawl in state,
Then folded her hands ridged with sinews and corded with veins,
Folded them across her breasts spent with the nourishing of children,
Gazed at the sky past the tops of the cedars,
Saw two spangled nights arise out of the twilight,
Saw two days go by filled with the tranquil sunshine,
Saw, without pain, or dread, or even a moment of longing:
Then on the third great night there came thronging and thronging
Millions of snowflakes out of a windless cloud;
They covered her close with a beautiful crystal shroud,
Covered her deep and silent.
But in the frost of the dawn,
Up from the life below,
Rose a column of breath
Through a tiny cleft in the snow,
Fragile, delicately drawn,
Wavering with its own weakness,
In the wilderness a sign of the spirit,
Persisting still in the sight of the sun
Till day was done.
Then all light was gathered up by the hand of God and hid in His breast,
Then there was born a silence deeper than silence,
Then she had rest.

The Ballad Tradition (Years 7-10)
Glenys Acland, Joe Belanger & Ken Watson

Several ballads are included in this volume, and thus there is an opportunity for a class to undertake an extended unit on the ballad tradition, starting with the old English and Scottish ballads *The Unquiet Grave* (p15), *The Golden Vanity* (pp20-22), *the Twa Corbies* and *The Three Ravens* (pp23-25). To these might be added the widely anthologised *Lord Randal* and *Edward, Edward*, which, like so many of the older ballads, are somewhat elliptical, even omitting the motivation for the crimes they recount. The students will soon become aware of the qualities defining these old ballads: simple story line (usually tragic), musical quality (most were sung), repetition, swiftness of action, omission of detail. They should be asked to decide how it is that these old ballads have survived so long, and when they move on to the ballads of the last two centuries they can see what characteristics of the old ballads are still to be found in the anonymous ballads of the 19th century and in the more 'literary' ballads of recent times.

When migrants came to North America and Australia they brought with them a fund of folk poetry and old ballads out of which grew bush songs with local settings celebrating, and often humorously reflecting on, the hazards of life in the new lands. And soon a literary movement developed: in North America with such writers as Bret Harte and Alexander McLachlan, and in Australia writers like Adam Lindsay Gordon, A B 'Banjo' Paterson, Will Ogilvie and Henry Lawson (though the reputation of the last depends much more upon his short stories).

This section begins with an anonymous ballad from Australia, *The Death of Ben Hall*. After Ned Kelly, Ben Hall was the best known of the 19th century bushrangers and, like Kelly, became a folk hero.

The most famous of the Australian literary ballads, 'Banjo' Paterson's *The Man From Snowy River* is too well known to be reprinted here (though teachers in other countries who cannot find it easily are welcome to write to St Clair Press for copies – the poem is out of copyright). Instead, a ballad by Will Ogilvie, who wrote in the early 20th century, is included, together with a recent humorous ballad by Kel Richards.

The Canadian equivalent of 'Banjo' Paterson is Robert Service, whose most famous ballad, *The Cremation of Sam McGee* is given here, together with another ballad arising from the Canadian ballad tradition, Robert Stead's *The Squad of One*. Detailed suggestions for treating these poems in class are given below, and teachers might, in addition, ask students to decide which of the two famous ballads, *The Man from Snowy River* and *The Cremation of Sam McGee*, is the more effective.

The Ballad Tradition

The Death Of Ben Hall
Anon.

Ben Hall was out on the Lachlan side
With a thousand pounds on his head;
A score of troopers were scattered wide
And a hundred more were ready to ride
Wherever a rumour led.

They had followed his track from the Weddin heights
And north by the Weelong yards;
Through dazzling days and moonlit nights
They had sought him over their rifle-sights,
With their hands on their trigger-guards.

The outlaw stole like a hunted fox
Through the scrub and stunted heath,
And peered like a hawk from his eyrie rocks
Through the waving boughs of the sapling box
On the troopers riding beneath.

His clothes were rent by the clutching thorn
And his blistered feet were bare;
Ragged and torn, with his beard unshorn,
He hid in the woods like a beast forlorn,
With a padded path to his lair.

But every night when the white stars rose
He crossed by the Gunning Plain
To a stockman's hut where the Gunning flows,
And struck on the door three swift light blows,
And a hand unhooked the chain –

And the outlaw followed the lone path back
With food for another day,
And the kindly darkness covered his track
And the shadows swallowed him deep and black
Where the starlight melted away.

But his friend had read of the Big Reward,
And his soul was stirred with greed;
He fastened his door and window-board,
He saddled his horse and crossed the ford,
And spurred to the town at speed.

You may ride at a man's or a maid's behest
When honour or true love call
And steel your heart to the worst or best,
But the ride that is ta'en on a traitor's quest
Is the bitterest ride of all.

A hot wind blew from the Lachlan bank
And a curse on its shoulder came;
The pine-trees frowned at him, rank on rank,
The sun on a gathering storm-cloud sank
And flushed his cheek with shame.

He reined at the Court; and the tale began
That the rifles alone should end;
Sergeant and trooper laid their plan
To draw the net on a hunted man
At the treacherous word of a friend.

False was the hand that raised the chain
And false was the whispered word:
"The troopers have turned to the south again,
You may dare to camp on the Gunning Plain."
And the weary outlaw heard.

He walked from the hut but a quarter-mile
Where a clump of saplings stood
In a sea of grass like a lonely isle;
And the moon came up in a little while
Like silver steeped in blood.

Ben Hall lay down on the dew-wet ground
By the side of his tiny fire;
And a night-breeze woke, and he heard no sound
As the troopers drew their cordon round –
And the traitor earned his hire.

And nothing they saw in the dim grey light,
But the little glow in the trees;
And they crouched in the tall cold grass all night,
Each one ready to shoot at sight,
With his rifle cocked on his knees.

When the shadows broke and the dawn's white sword
Swung over the mountain wall,
And a little wind blew over the ford,
A sergeant sprang to his feet and roared:
"In the name of the Queen, Ben Hall!"

Haggard, the outlaw leapt from his bed
With his lean arms held on high.
"Fire!" And the word was scarcely said
When the mountains rang to a rain of lead –
And the dawn went drifting by.

They kept their word and they paid his pay
Where a clean man's hand would shrink;
And that was the traitor's master-day
As he stood by the bar on his homeward way
And called on the crowd to drink.

He banned no creed and he barred no class,
And he called to his friends by name;
But the worst would shake his head and pass
And none would drink from the bloodstained glass
And the goblet red with shame.

And I know when I hear the last grim call
And my mortal hour is spent,
When the light is hid and the curtains fall
I would rather sleep with the dead Ben Hall
Than go where that traitor went.

How The Fire Queen Crossed The Swamp

Will Ogilvie

The flood was down in the Wilga swamps, three feet over the mud,
And the teamsters camped on the Wilga range and swore at the rising flood;
For one by one they had tried the trip, double and treble teams,
And one after one each desert-ship had dropped to her axle-beams;
So they thonged their leaders and pulled them round to the camp on the sandhill's crown,
And swore by the bond of a blood-red oath to wait till the floods went down.

There were side-rail tubs and table-tops, coaches and bullock-drays,
Brawn with the Barcoo Wonders, and Speed with the dapple grays
Who pulled the front of his wagon out and left the rest in the mud
At the Cuttaburra crossing in the grip of the Ninety flood.
There was Burt with his sixteen bullocks, and never a bullock to shirk,
Who twice came over the border line with twelve-ton-ten to Bourke;
There was Long Dick damning an agent's eyes for his ton of extra weight,
And Whistling Jim, for Cobb and Co, cursing that mails were late,
And one blasphemed at a broken chain and howled for a blacksmith's blood,
And most of them cursed their crimson luck, and all of them cursed the flood.

The last of the baffled had struggled back and the sun was low in the sky,
And the first of the stars was creeping out when Dareaway Dan came by.
There's never a teamster draws to Bourke but has taken the help of Dan;
There's never a team on the Great North Road can lift as the big roans can:
Broad-hipped beauties that nothing can stop, leaders that swing to a cough;
Eight blue-roans on the near side yoked, and eight red-roans on the off.
And Long Dick called from his pine-rail bunk: "Where are you bound so quick?"
And Dareaway Dan spoke low to the roans, and aloud "To the Swagman's, Dick!"
"There's five good miles," said the giant, "lie to the front of you, holding mud;
If you never were stopped before, old man, you are stopped by the Wilga flood.
The dark will be down in an hour or so, there isn't the ghost of a moon;
So leave your nags in the station grass instead of the long lagoon!"

But Dan stood up to the leader's head and fondled the big brown nose:
"There's many a mile in the roan team yet before they are fed for the crows;
Now listen, Dick-with-the-woman's-heart, a word to you and the rest:
I've sixteen horses collared and chained, the pick of the whole wide West,
And I'll cut their throats and leave them here to rot if they haven't the power
To carry me through the gates of Hell – with seventy bags of flour!
The light of the stars is light enough; they have nothing to do but plough;
There's never a swamp has held them yet, and a swamp won't stop them now.
They're waiting for flour at the Swagman's Bend; I'll steer for the lifting light;
There's nothing to fear with a team like mine, and – I camp in the bend tonight!"

So they stood aside and they watched them pass in the glow of the sinking sun,
With straining muscles and tightened chains – sixteen pulling like one;
With jingling harness and droning wheels and bare hoofs' rhythmic tramp,
With creaking timbers and lurching load the Fire Queen faced the swamp!
She dipped her red shafts low in the slush as a spoonbill dips her beak,
The black mud clung to the wheels and fell in the wash of the Wilga creek;
And the big roans fought for footing, and the spreaders threshed like flails,
And the great wheels lifted the muddy spume to the bend of the red float-rails;
And they cheered him out to the westward with the last of the failing light
And the splashing hoofs and the driver's voice died softly away in the night;
And some of them prate of a shadowy form that guided the leader's reins,
And some of them speak of a shod black horse that pulled in the off-side chains –
How every time that he lifted his feet the wagon would groan and swing,
And every time that he dropped his head you could hear the tug-chains ring!

And Dan to the Swagman's Bend came through mud-spattered from foot to head,
And they couldn't tell which of the roans were blue and which of the roans were red.
Now this is the tale as I heard it told, and many believe it true
When the teamsters say in their off-hand way – "Twas the Devil that pulled him through!"

The Ballad Of Percival Pig

Kel Richards

Once, I called into a pig farm,
(I sold insurance door to door).
There were lots of tiny piglets,
Some sows and one big boar.

Now, believe me, that big male pig,
(I really saw it, last July),
That pig...it had a wooden leg!
(Truly! Would I lie?)

I told the farmer what I saw,
"Yeah, that's my Percival," he said.
"Old Percival's me only pig,
That's got a wooden leg."

Sitting down he told the story,
Of that quite amazing pig,
The tale of its intelligence,
And all the things it did.

STUDENTS' PAGE

"You see those oil wells over there?
Percy told us where to put 'em,
And when the bills was mountin' up,
He told us how to foot 'em.

"By dredging in the creek for gold,
Then buying stocks and bonds and shares.
Although in trading currency,
His judgement's only fair."

I looked at him quite doubtfully,
(Well, I ask you; wouldn't you?)
So the farmer got all cranky,
And swore that it was true.

"If you really don't believe me,
Then you're the one that's loony:
Perce has earned a Law Degree,
From the Law School (Sydney Uni.)

"In all the world no other pig,
Is near as bright as Percy,
As well as all that IQ,
He's got courage, grit and mercy.

One night this house caught fire,
An inferno blazed about,
Into the flames dashed Percy,
And pulled us safely out.

Oh yes, he really saved my life,
And my wife and baby Peg."
And then I asked the farmer
About Percy's wooden leg.

"Do I really look that stupid, son?
Do you take me for a dunce?
With a pig as smart as Percy,
You don't eat it all at once."

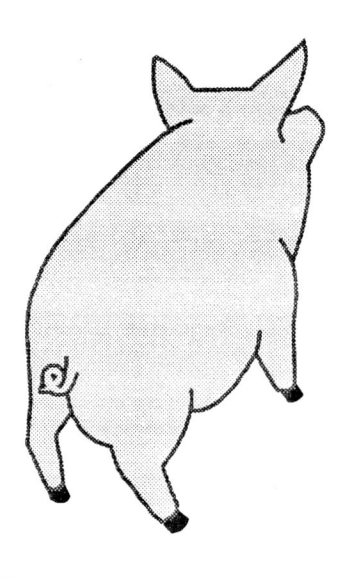

My Best Poetry Unit

Writing a Ballad

A common pattern in ballads – so common it is sometimes called **ballad metre** – is the four-line stanza in which the first and third lines have four stressed syllables and the second and fourth three stresses, with these two lines rhyming:

> The anchor broke, the topmast split,
>   'Twas such a deadly storm,
> The waves came over the broken ship
>   Till all her sides were torn.
>
> *Sir Patrick Spens*

In your group, decide on a story that would make a good ballad (eg, a sporting event like a football or hockey match, the sinking of the *Titanic*, a driving lesson where things go wrong). Using ballad metre, construct the first stanza, and then plan what each of the remaining five, six, seven stanzas will be about. After you have planned the ballad, write the remaining stanzas.

Prepare an illustrated poster of your ballad for display in the classroom.

TEACHER'S PAGE

Two Canadian Ballads

The Squad of One by Robert Stead and *The Cremation of Sam McGee* by Robert W Service. These two narrative poems offer insights into the lives of the pioneers who opened the Canadian West. However, while *The Squad of One* is grounded in historical events, *The Cremation of Sam McGee* is the product of the poet's imagination. These poems have a number of features in common (Canadian-American rivalry; struggles with a harsh environment; loneliness and isolation), but they are quite different in some respects (eg, Service presents a tall tale of life in the far North while Stead tells the story of a Mounted Police Officer using his wits to overcome odds).

The Squad of One

The Squad of One is based on a story which was told to Robert Stead by a NWMP corporal when Stead was a young man. Although the names and geographical details have been changed, the essence of the story is true. Students interested in the history of the Royal Canadian Mounted Police might look up the RCMP web page (www.rcmp-grc.gc.ca click on link "about the RCMP") or read the biographies of such early Mounted Police officers as Sir Samuel Benfield Steele or James F McLeod.

Students may be familiar with the motto "The Mounties always get their man". The Force prides itself on persistence, but also on cunning and common sense, as the poem illustrates.

Activities

1. Stead writes *Squad ...* from the point of view of Sergeant Blue. There are, of course, different points of view in any story. Students might tell the story from the point of view of one of the "toughs" who is, perhaps, sitting in a jail cell in Montana, telling his new cellmate how he was captured. Alternatively, US Marshall Jack McMann might give an interview to a reporter from a Montana newspaper about how two toughs who were wanted "dead or alive" were captured in a foreign country. (Or, if you want to jump a hundred years ahead, a radio or TV interview.)

2. Deeds such as the capture of the toughs by Sergeant Blue are also easy to spoof. Students might create short dramas which exaggerate Jack McMann's language and attitudes toward shooting people – one which makes him look foolish; one which makes him look brilliant. Alternatively, Sergeant Blue might be cast as the seemingly bumbling Lieutenant Columbo, from the TV program of the same name.

3. The fifteen stanza poem works well as readers' theatre. Pairs of students can be assigned one or two stanzas to read aloud (in chorus) to the class. Alternatively, students might act out segments of the poem: Sergeant Blue's reading of the letter from Jack McMann and his speculations on how he will capture the felons make a good soliloquy; the incident in the homesteader's shack provides the opportunity to fill in the action with dialogue.

4. Students might explore the verse form used in the poem. Why is this verse form appropriate or inappropriate for telling this story? What is the effect of the long lines?

5. On the basis of the story line, language, rhythm, rhyme, narrative elements, and imagery, decide whether you prefer *The Squad of One* or *The Cremation of Sam McGee*.

Vocabulary

Students might benefit from being told the meanings of such words as:

Snake Creek Bend: a fictional RCMP post on the Canadian prairies. Okatoks, on the other hand, is a small town in Southern Alberta.

homestead: a parcel of land in the Canadian West, usually about a quarter section of land (160 acres) which was granted to settlers under certain conditions in the late 1800s.

fighting irons: handguns.

horn of the best: a bottle of liquor, probably moonshine.

halter shank: a piece of rope under two metres in length which is tied to a leather headstall, used for securing or leading animals.

The Cremation of Sam McGee

Introduction

The Cremation of Sam McGee, with its internal rhyme and galloping rhythm, races along. Since the poem is relatively easy to understand on a basic level, one good way to introduce it is to read it aloud. A first oral reading might uncover the plot while a second reading might focus on the ways that the poet achieves the poem's effects.

The Cremation of Sam McGee is so well known in Canada that many who have studied English in Canadian schools can recite at least the first stanza. It is worth lingering on the first stanza to savour the rhythm and rhyme and to explore how the poet sets up the remainder of the poem in the first verse. Indeed, the first verse is repeated verbatim as the final verse, almost as a chorus. Students might list words which foreshadow mystery and surprise and describe ways they prepare the reader for the title event.

Activities

The Story Line

In this tall tale, the reader is prepared in various ways to accept the idea that Sam McGee could sit in the centre of a raging fire and ask that the furnace door be closed to keep in the heat. Beginning with the picture of mystery and surprise painted in the opening stanza, students can trace the events that prepare them for Sam's weathering the fiery furnace. What plausible events does Service present to give the story credibility?

The Language

The language of *Sam McGee* appears to be more sophisticated and less conversational than that used in *The Squad of One*. Students might compare the diction and the use of colloquial language in the two poems and explore their effects.

The Narrator
Service tells the story of Sam McGee from the point of view of a first-person narrator. What are the effects of this type of report? What would be the effect of telling it from the "objective" point of view? How might Sam McGee himself tell the story? What would he leave out?

Sam McGee also lends itself to readers' theatre and to choral speaking. Groups of students might also dramatise specific scenes from the poem.

Other Service Poems
Students who enjoyed *Sam McGee* might be interested in reading other tall tales written by Robert W Service: *The Ballad of the Iceworm Cocktail* tells the story of a prank played on an English remittance man, Major Percy Brown, as he tried to gain acceptance and become a bonafide Yukon pioneer; *The Shooting of Dan McGrew* reports a love affair gone sour; *The Men That Don't Fit In* explores the reasons people seek the isolation of Canada's far north.

Biographical notes on Robert W Service and the texts of many of his poems are found on the web at <http://selfknowledge.com/spyuk11.htm>.

Sam McGee Illustrated
Service, Robert W, and Harrison, Ted (1907/1986). *The Cremation of Sam McGee*, Toronto, Ontario: Kids Can Press. This picture book illustrates the poem, but the graphics frequently go beyond the poem to illustrate life in Canada's North.

Vocabulary:
Students might require help with some of the vocabulary from Canada's North.
Mushing: a journey made by dogsled, especially walking on snowshoes behind a dog sled.
Dawson Trail: Dawson City, Yukon, was the centre of the Yukon Gold Rush in 1898; Service wrote "The Cremation ..." in 1907, not long after the Gold Rush.
Marge: edge, shore (margin).
Moil: drudgery; from Old French to moisten or paddle in the mud.
Midnight Sun: in the high Arctic the sun stays above the horizon 24 hours per day in late June and early July.

Students might find it interesting that both the derelict "Alice May" and Lake Labarge are factual.

The Squad Of One

Robert Stead

Sergeant Blue of the Mounted Police was a so-so kind of guy;
He swore a bit, and he lied a bit, and he boozed a bit on the sly;
But he held the post at Snake Creek Bend in the good old British way,
And a grateful country paid him about sixty cents a day.

Now the life of the North-West Mounted Police breeds an all-round kind of man;
A man who can finish whatever he starts, and no matter how it began;
A man who can wrestle a drunken bum, or break up a range stampede-
Such are the men of the Mounted Police, and such are the men they breed.

The snow lay deep at the Snake Creek post and deep to east and west,
And the Sergeant had made his ten-league beat and settled down to rest
In his two-by-four that they called a "post", where the flag flew overhead,
And he took a look at his monthly mail, and this is the note he read:

"To Sergeant Blue, of the Mounted Police, at the post at Snake Creek Bend,
From U.S. Marshal of County Blank, greetings to you, my friend:
They's a team of toughs give us the slip, though they shot up a couple of blokes,
And we reckon they's hid in Snake Creek Gulch, and posin' as farmer folks.

"Of all the toughs I ever saw I reckon these the worst,
So shoot to kill if you shoot at all, and be sure you do it first,
And send out your strongest squad of men and round them up if you can,
For dead of alive we want them here. Yours truly, Jack McMann."

And Sergeant Blue sat back and smiled, and his heart was glad and free,
And he said, "If I round these beggars up it's another stripe for me;
And promotion don't come easy to one of us Mounty chaps,
So I'll scout around tomorrow and I'll bring them in – perhaps."

Next morning Sergeant Blue, arrayed in farmer smock and jeans,
In a jumper sleigh he had made himself set out for the evergreens
That grow on the bank of Snake Creek Gulch by a homestead shack he knew,
And a smoke curled up from the chimney-pipe to welcome Sergeant Blue.

"Aha!" said Blue, "and who are you? Behold, the chimney smokes,
But the boy that owns this homestead shack is up at Okotoks;
And he wasn't expecting callers, for he left his key with me,
So I'll just drop in for an interview and we'll see what we shall see!"

So he drove his horse to the shanty door and hollered a loud "Good day,"
And a couple of men with fighting-irons came out beside the sleigh;
And the Sergeant said, "I'm a stranger here and I've driven a weary mile,
If you don't object I'll just sit down by the stove in the shack for a while."

Then the Sergeant sat and smoked and talked of the home he had left down East,
And the cold and the snow, and the price of land, and the life of man and beast,
But all of sudden he broke if off with, "Neighbours, take a nip?
There's a horn of the best you'll find out there in my jumper, in the grip."

So one of the two went out for it, and as soon as he closed the door
The Sergeant tickled the other one's ribs with the nose of his forty-four;
"Now, fellow," he said, "you're a man of sense, and you know when you're on the rocks,
And a noise as loud as a mouse from you and they'll take you home in a box."

And he fastened the bracelets to his wrists, and his legs with a halter-shank,
And he took his knife and he took his gun and he made him safe as the bank,
And then he mustered Number Two in an Indian file parade,
And he gave some brief directions – and Number Two obeyed.

And when he had coupled them each to each and set them down on the bed,
"It's a frosty day and we'd better eat before we go," he said.
So he fried some pork and he warmed some beans, and he set out the best he saw,
And he noted the price for the man of the house, according to British law.

That night in the post sat Sergeant Blue, with paper and pen in hand,
And this is the word he wrote and signed and mailed to a foreign land:
"To U.S. Marshal of County Blank, greetings I give to you;
My squad has just brought in your men, and the squad was Sergeant Blue."

There are things unguessed, there are tales untold, in the life of the great lone land,
But here is a fact that the prairie-bred alone may understand,
That a thousand miles in the fastnesses the fear of the law obtains,
And the pioneers of justice were the "Riders of the Plains".

The Cremation Of Sam Mcgee

Robert Service

There are strange things done in the midnight sun
By the men who moil for gold;
The Arctic trails have their secret tales
That would make your blood run cold;
The Northern Lights have seen queer sights,
But the queerest they ever did see
Was that night on the marge of Lake Lebarge
I cremated Sam McGee.

Now Sam McGee was from Tennessee, where the cotton blooms and blows.
Why he left his home in the South to roam 'round the Pole, God only knows.
He was always cold, but the land of gold seemed to hold him like a spell;
Though he'd often say in his homely way that "he'd sooner live in hell".
On a Christmas Day we were mushing our way over the Dawson trail.
Talk of your cold! through the parka's fold it stabbed like a driven nail.
If our eyes we'd close, then the lashes froze till sometimes we couldn't see;
It wasn't much fun, but the only one to whimper was Sam McGee.

And that very night, as we lay packed tight in our robes beneath the snow,
And the dogs were fed, and the stars o'erhead were dancing heel and toe,
He turned to me, and "Cap," says he, "I'll cash in this trip, I guess;
And if I do, I'm asking that you won't refuse my last request."

STUDENTS' PAGE

Well, he seemed so low that I couldn't say no; then he says with a sort of moan:
"It's the cursed cold, and it's got right hold till I'm chilled clean through to the bone.
Yet 'tain't being dead – it's my awful dread of the icy grave that pains;
So I want you to swear that, foul or fair, you'll cremate my last remains."

A pal's last need is a thing to heed, so I swore I would not fail;
And we started on at the streak of dawn; but God! he looked ghastly pale.
He crouched on the sleigh, and he raved all day of his home in Tennessee;
And before nightfall a corpse was all that was left of Sam McGee.
There wasn't a breath in that land of death, and I hurried, horror driven,
With a corpse half hid that I couldn't get rid, because of a promise given;
It was lashed to the sleigh, and it seemed to say: "You may tax your brawn and brains,
But you promised true, and it's up to you to cremate those last remains."

Now a promise made is a debt unpaid, and the trail has its own stern code.
In the days to come, though my lips were dumb, in my heart how I cursed that load.
In the long, long night, but the long firelight, whiles the huskies, round in a ring,
Howled out their woes to the homeless snows – O God! how I loathed the thing!

And every day that quiet clay seemed to heavy and heavier grow;
And on I went, though the dogs were spent and the grub was getting low;
The trail was bad, and I felt half mad, but I swore I would not give in;
And I'd often sing to the hateful thing, and it hearkened with a grin.

Till I came to the marge of Lake Lebarge, and a derelict there lay;
It was jammed in the ice, but I saw in a trice it was called the "Alice May".
And I looked at it, and I thought a bit, and I looked at my frozen chum;
Then "Here," said I, with a sudden cry, "is my cre-ma-tor-eum."

Some planks I tore from the cabin floor, and I lit the boiler fire;
Some coal I found that was lying around, and I heaped the fuel higher;
The flames just soared, and the furnace roared – such a blaze you seldom see;
And I burrowed a hole in the glowing coal, and I stuffed in Sam McGee.

Then I made a hike, for I didn't like to hear him sizzle so;
And the heavens scowled, and the huskies howled, and the wind began to blow.
It was icy cold, but the hot sweat rolled down my cheeks, and I don't know why;
And the greasy smoke in an inky cloak went streaking down the sky.

I do not know how long in the snow I wrestled with grisly fear;
But the stars came out and they danced about ere again I ventured near;
I was sick with dread, but I bravely said: "I'll just take a peep inside.
I guess he's cooked, and it's time I looked,"...then the door I opened wide.

And there sat Sam, looking cool and calm, in the heart of the furnace roar;
And he wore a smile you could see a mile, and he said: "Please close that door.
It's fine in here, but I greatly fear you'll let in the cold and storm –
Since I left Plumtree, down in Tennessee, it's the first time I've been warm."

There are strange things done in the midnight sun
By the men who moil for gold;
The Arctic trails have their secret tales
That would make your blood run cold;
The Northern Lights have seen queer sights,
But the queerest they ever did see
Was that night on the marge of Lake Lebarge
I cremated Sam McGee.

Answers and Imitations: Exploring Tone (Years 10-12)
Ken Watson

Some poems have so captured the imaginations of other poets that they have imitated, answered and sometimes the parodied the originals. When Christopher Marlowe published *The Passionate Shepherd to His Love*, for example, Sir Walter Raleigh immediately penned *The Nymph's Reply to the Shepherd*.

Sir Richard Lovelace's poem, *To Lucasta, Going to the Warres*, has inspired poets of succeeding ages, perhaps because the paradox on which it turns is one that almost every generation has faced since. Lovelace (1618-58), was the most prominent of the Cavalier poets, writers who graced the court of King Charles I and who fought on the Royalist side in the English Civil War. The poem is often seen as embodying the ideals of the Cavaliers, who were described by Sellar and Yeatman in their comic *1066 and All That* as "wrong but romantic" (in contrast to the Puritans, who were "right but repulsive"!).

Lucasta was Lovelace's fiancée, Lucy Sacheverell. After receiving a false report of his death, she married someone else.

A comparison between Lovelace's poem on the one hand, and on the other the poems of two soldier-poets of the 20th century, Robert Graves (First World War) and John Manifold (Second World War) allows students to explore the concept of tone, or attitude conveyed.

It is suggested that students, in groups, discuss the attitude to going off to war conveyed in Lovelace's poem, and then discuss the somewhat different tone of Manifold's poem. The stark contrast in tone between the Lovelace and Graves poems is probably best left until last, even though the latter was written a generation earlier than Manifold's.

John Manifold – Australian poet who fought with the British Army during the Second World War.

One dies at Zutphen – Sir Philip Sidney died of wounds received in a minor engagement at Zutphen the Low Countries in 1586.

One in Greece – Lord Byron. Rupert Brooke also died on a ship off the Greek island of Skyros on the way to Gallipoli in 1915.

Dozens in France and Spain – including Wilfred Owen and Isaac Rosenberg in France during the First World War, and Frederico Garcia Lorca in Spain shortly after the outbreak of the Spanish Civil War.

Greece's turn again – in 1941 British and Australian troops tried unsuccessfully to prevent the German occupation of Greece and Crete.

Robert Graves – throughout the First World War Robert Graves was an officer in the Royal Welch Fusiliers. His autobiography, *Good-bye to All That*, graphically describes this part of his life.

For the fourth time – returning to the Front for the fourth time after leave in England.

TEACHER'S PAGE

In his *A Book of Answers* (1978), the Australian poet A D Hope picks up on the 17th century fondness for 'answers' to poems, and provides, amongst others, answers to Ben Jonson's *To Celia* (Drink to me Only...), to Donne's *The Sun Rising* and Marvell's *To His Coy Mistress*. In his introduction to *Lucasta's Reply to Mr Richard Lovelace* he argues that Lovelace's poem "has suffered from being taken too seriously by many readers who have missed its delicate parody of the courtly love conventions. It is plainly meant to make Lucasta laugh away her tears and remonstrances: but if she laughed, as a girl of spirit she might well have been tempted to reply in kind."

This view could be put to the class after they have explored the contrasting tones of the previous three poems.

Finally, the students can enjoy Guiterman's light-hearted parody, and perhaps try their hands at their own imitations, answers or parodies.

To Lucasta, Going To The Warres

Richard Lovelace

Tell me not (Sweet) I am unkinde,
That from the Nunnerie
Of thy chaste breast, and quiet minde,
To Warre and Armes I flie.

True; a new Mistresse now I chase,
The first Foe in the Field;
And with a stronger Faith imbrace
A Sword, a Horse, a Shield.

Yet this Inconstancy is such,
As you too shall adore;
I could not love thee (Deare) so much,
Lov'd I not Honour more.

To Lucasta

On seeing no immediate hope of returning from the wars

John Manifold

The facts may be a bit obscure
But all the legends show
A poet's blood is good manure
Where freedom is to grow.

One dies at Zutphen, one in Greece,
Dozens in France and Spain,
And now it looks, by all one reads,
Like Greece's turn again.

The mode is exigent, my sweet;
I cannot well refuse
To stoop and buckle to my feet
My pair of dead men's shoes.

To Lucasta On Going To The Wars –
For The Fourth Time

Robert Graves

It doesn't matter what's the cause,
What wrong they say we're righting,
A curse for treaties, bonds and laws,
When we're to do the fighting!
And since we lads are proud and true,
What else remains to do?
Lucasta, when to France your man
Returns his fourth time, hating war,
Yet laughs as calmly as he can
And flings an oath, but says no more,
That is not courage, that's not fear –
Lucasta he's a Fusilier,
And his pride sends him here.

Let statesmen bluster, bark and bray
And so decide who started
This bloody war, and who's to pay
But he must be stout-hearted,
Must sit and stake with quiet breath,
Playing at cards with Death.
Don't plume yourself he fights for you;
It is not courage, love or hate
That lets us do the things we do;
It's pride that makes the heart so great;
It is not anger, no, nor fear -
Lucasta he's a Fusilier,
And his pride keeps him here.

Lucasta's Reply To Mr Richard Lovelace

A D Hope

The answer thou return'st me, Dick,
Doth prove thee still unkind,
To try by sophisms to trick
This quiet, but lucid, mind.

If a new mistress now you chase,
What care I who she be?
'Tis not the horse but the embrace
That still displeaseth me.

Can Honour then on Love forestall?
Or needs it such repair?
I had not loved thee, dear, at all
Hadst thou been wanting there.

Alibi

Arthur Guiterman

Blame me not, Sweet, if here and there
My wayward self inclines
To note that others, too, are fair,
To bow at lesser shrines.

What though with eye or tongue I praise
Iona's gentle wile,
Camilla's happy turn of phrase,
Or Celia's winning smile?

My constancy shall be thy boast
From now to Kingdom Come.
How could I love thee, Dear, the most,
Loved I not others, some?

TEACHER'S PAGE

Life Matters (Years 10-12) — Roslyn Arnold

These poems work because a familiar phrase or question ('Dear Sir, we thank you'; 'How's that?') is used as the framework. This allows the poet to contrast the commonplace/ordinary with the more serious or profound. The contrast is often subtle and supported by an ironic tone of voice.

The students could try taking a common phrase (eg, 'G'day, mate'; 'What's up?'; 'How's things?'; 'As if I care') and see if they can apply it to a person or context for clever effect. It would help if they can think of someone unexpected using the phrase, as, say, an elderly woman saying 'G'day, mate!'. What if she did so?

Another poem that could be grouped with these three is F T Macartney's *Bargain Basement* (page 16).

Life Matters

Yours Sincerely

Barry Cole

Dear Sir, we thank you for your
application and are pleased
to offer you a lease of
not less than seventy years
(four-score-and-ten seems the rule).

We hope you appreciate
the value of our loan and
will remit such interest
as falls due (we're familiar
with the advent of your birth).

You'll understand, of course, that
when we say "lease" we don't mean
"left alone". The opposite:
we convey a contract, say
or imply you're one of ours.

Without such a rider we
would tumble, upset ancient
precedent, perhaps suggest
that man, despite his faults, is
to coin a word, immortal.

Please sign your name in the space
provided. This will confirm
that you are born of woman
and will, when your time comes, go
in such peace as when you came.

Lending Library

David King

Yes, young sir, your new membership
Is a lifetime one. Now, what
Do you wish to take out?

The Promise of Happiness? An excellent
    choice,
Though you'll find, I fear,
That promises are fragile,
Fleeting as shadows.

Ah, young sir, you're
Back. And your new book?
Wider Horizons – an interesting choice;
The world's your oyster – ha ha.

Ah, sir, a pleasure to see you
Again. *Sweetest Melancholy*?
Could it be
That you're in love?

Your choice today?
The Optimist?
"Greet the unseen with a cheer,"
As Browning says.

Ah, sir, we haven't see you
For some time. *Outrageous Fortune*?
Surely there's hope
For possibility or surprise.

Your final choice, I think.
No Traveller Returns – yes,
We may be reasonably sure
Of that.

How's that?

Norman Nicholson

How's that?
Asks the bowler –
Pad before wicket,
Feet splayed awry, wrist higher
Than shoulder, a comic cartoon of cricket –
Not out
Says the Umpire.

How's that?
Ask the Neighbours –
Sacked from his job with the Dole Queue for a hobby,
Cheques bounced by the Bank, wife
Run off with the lodger, bailiff's in the lobby –
Not out,
Says Life.

How's that?
Asks the Justice –
Nabbed red-handed, stranded with no hope,
And a hundred willing hands ready to shove
A branded man still lower down the slope –
Not out,
Says Love.

How's that?
Asks the Doctor –
Four score years and ten,
With a gurgle in the bronchials, a growling in the breath,
Appealing for a re-play, life over once again –
Out
Says Death.